# Meat Cleaver Man and Other Stories of the Post-Soviet Space

# Meat Cleaver Man and Other Stories of the Post-Soviet Space

Teresa Wigglesworth-Baker

Copyright © 2024 Teresa Wigglesworth-Baker
All rights reserved.

All photographs Copyright © 2024 Teresa Wigglesworth-Baker

All rights reserved.

**ISBN:** 9798320568218

# Contents

Introduction _____ 1

Part 1: The Soviet Union _____ 7

    Chapter 1: The School Exchange Trip _____ 8

Chapter 2: The Transition to the Post-Soviet Space ____ 21

    Part 2: Latvia _____ 31

    Chapter 3: Arrival _____ 32

    Chapter 4: Meat Cleaver Man _____ 40

    Chapter 5: Richie Blackmore _____ 44

    Chapter 6: Family Feast _____ 46

Part 3: The Closed Administrative Territories of the Soviet Union _____ 51

    Chapter 7: Kaliningrad aka Korolev - The Soviet Space Flight Control Centre _____ 55

    Chapter 8: The Great Escape - from Dubna _____ 63

Part 4: The Republic of Tatarstan _____ 71

    Chapter 9: Visa Registration in Kazan _____ 74

    Chapter 10: Stock Cubes _____ 99

Part 5: Georgia _____ 109

    Chapter 11: The Banya _____ 113

    Chapter 12: Health and Safety _____ 122

    Chapter 12: The Cat Lady of Sioni Street, Tbilisi __ 133

Part 6: Ukraine _____ 143

    Chapter 13: Food for Thought _____ 144

Endnotes _____ 157

Further Reading _____ 161

Author bio _____ 164

**Introduction**

This book is a self-reflective ethnography of short travel stories, which began during the late Soviet period, through the collapse of the USSR and continues up to the present day across the post-Soviet space.

The narrative of the book is mainly contextualized within Charles Forsdick's definitions of horizontal and vertical travel[1]. Horizontal travel is considered to be the linear conventional aspect of travel where the traveller moves from place to place. In terms of this book, the horizontal narrative follows the chronological order of trips I made to the Soviet and post-Soviet spaces.

Vertical travel, on the other hand, is about movement downwards or underground and allows the traveller an insight into spaces, which are either hidden from or unnoticed by the conventional traveller. In other words, it is what is not usually apparent or is stumbled upon, or as I term, a per happenstance, a coincidence. These coincidences can make the lived experiences frightening, exciting and richer at the same time. The vertical travel therefore forms the basis for each chapter in this book.

The horizontal travels thus begin in Leningrad, Donetsk, and then Moscow during the Soviet period on a school exchange trip in 1984. I went on this trip because I was studying Russian at school. Later, I continued to study Russian and French at university in London and went to spend a compulsory year abroad of language immersion, firstly in Paris, and then in Riga, Latvia in 1992-93. After graduating, I went to work in Moscow's satellite towns and in Moscow itself for a few years teaching English as a foreign language. Many years later, after teaching in other countries of eastern Europe, I returned to Sheffield where I continued teaching, but couldn't get the language and travel bug out of my system and so I studied for a Master's degree researching the language situation in Belarus. Following this, I continued research work into language and identity in the post-Soviet space by studying for a doctorate. I examined language policy and Russian-titular language use in the Republic of Tatarstan and worked for the Tatar government as a language policy consultant for some time at the same time as my doctoral studies. After receiving my PhD in 2015, I went to work as an international expert for the Organisation for Security and Co-operation in Europe

(OSCE) and the Georgian Ministry of Education and Science. In Georgia I worked on multilingual education reforms for the Azeri and Armenian ethnic minorities residing in Georgia. Finally, I introduce the readers to virtual travel in Ukraine. All of these spaces have offered me insight into not only the history of this vast space, but also the political, economic, and socio-cultural underpinnings of this society.

Each of the stories comprises a coincidence that happened to me while I was either studying, working, or researching within the Soviet and post-Soviet spaces. In addition, I weave little known facts and information into each story for the reader. Each coincidence is multisensory as I invite the reader to see the space around me, smell and taste the cuisine of the countries visited and to hear the stories from the people who I had the chance to meet.

As a proficient speaker of Russian, I was able to understand the culture and gather much information about the issues that people were facing in their environments and relate this throughout my storytelling. By inviting the reader into these spaces, I also invite the reader to contemplate their own lived experiences and vertical travel.

I must point out, however, that the intention of these stories is not to give a political commentary for the reader, but to look more at the *everyday* within the spaces visited. The meaning of *everyday* used within these stories is based on Jean-Didier Urbain's[2] dichotomy of *exotic* versus *endotic*. His *exotic* refers to the geographical environment that a traveller visits, which is largely unknown, and which could be either somewhere near home or abroad, whereas the *endotic* is the everyday. The *everyday* has many meanings within this book. Firstly, it pertains to the *everyday* tasks I carried out within the environmental space such as study, work, and research. Secondly, it is also about how I became part of this *everyday* space and how I adapted to the environments and issues I faced as part of myself 'transitioning' into this space. Finally, it is about the *everyday* of the people I met and the *everyday* of their lives that were shared with me.

For more information about the political situation in the Soviet and post-Soviet spaces, I have provided a bibliography which lists works of interest for the reader, including some of my own academic publications about language and identity in the post-Soviet space.

On a final note, if there was a theme tune to this book, it would be anything by *Boney M*. Everywhere I have been and whatever situation I found myself in, there was always a *Boney M* track playing somewhere in the background, whether on a car radio in the Caucasus on my way to a school to interview teachers, at a disco, walking down a street or even in a post-office. The music was everywhere! So, if you can listen to music and read at the same time, download some *Boney M* and it will take you right to the very essence of my experiences. Enjoy!

*Teresa Wigglesworth-Baker January 2024*

# Part 1

# The Soviet Union

## Chapter 1: The School Exchange Trip

*November 1983*

*Dear Parent,*

<u>*A proposed visit to Sheffield's twin town, Donetsk, USSR*</u>

*Sheffield's Town Twinning Panel seems keen to encourage and support a visit to Donetsk for pupils studying Russian. I have been asked to provide some estimate of interest, and I would, therefore, be grateful for a response. I set down below as many details as have as yet emerged about the proposal.*

**Date** – *not yet determined, but possibly the first fortnight in July 1984.*

**Group** – *pupils mostly from Firth Park and Ecclesfield Schools, numbering in all about 30, accompanied by Russian speaking staff from these two schools.*

**Outline** – *London – Moscow by air. Two nights in Moscow.*

        *Moscow – Donetsk by air or rail. 1 week in Donetsk in a pioneer camp.*

        *Donetsk – Leningrad by air or rail. Two nights in Leningrad.*

        *Leningrad – London by air.*

*Cost –*    *This would probably work out at about £300 excluding incidentals, but it is probable that substantial support will be available from the city for this pilot visit, so that the cost to parents will be about £100 for each child.*

*Yours faithfully,*

*G. HARTLEY,*

*Headmaster.*

In 1984 I had been studying Russian at Firth Park Comprehensive School in Sheffield for about two years. I was fourteen years old. This year marked my first ever trip abroad, by plane, by myself (without family for the first time) to the Soviet Union. This trip was the pinnacle of my school years and subsequent life direction. It all began with the letter above, to all parents of children studying Russian.

I can't remember why I chose to study Russian at school – perhaps it was the excitement of learning about a closed, forbidden country, or the possibility of cracking the seemingly secret code of the Cyrillic alphabet. It was partly because I was excellent at languages and used to score one hundred per cent in all my French exams, obviously demonstrating a talent for languages. It was also because by learning Russian, I would escape the school bullies who weren't deemed intelligent enough to learn Russian and were placed in German language learning classes instead. It was a good choice, whatever the reason.

Sheffield was first twinned with Donetsk in 1956 after World War II. It is thought that Sheffield was the first city in the UK to be officially twinned with a Soviet city. The two cities were twinned to promote peace and friendship and several sporting and cultural events between the two cities were developed. Both cities had much in common – they were both mining and steel cities.

The trip to the Soviet Union was a pilot scheme offered by Sheffield City Council and was supposed to offer a tremendous opportunity for real contact and understanding between the two cultures. The intention of the trip, according to Sheffield City Council's Chief Education Officer of the time, was:

> *"...to make this very much a <u>working</u> visit and the students [us] would undertake to regard it as such. They [the students] would also need to be physically fit in order to enjoy the fairly rigorous activities involved: a pioneer camp is by no means a holiday camp in our sense!"*

Had the Chief Education Officer been there?! Well, whatever. It was going to be an adventure in any case. The itinerary was a little different to the original. We were to leave Sheffield Pond Street Bus Station on a coach to Gatwick, taking a packed lunch with us. We were to depart from Gatwick airport on 10$^{th}$ July at 16:00 on an Aeroflot fight SU1638 and arrive in Leningrad at 22:30 local time. On 11$^{th}$ July we were going to catch a flight to Donetsk and stay until Wednesday 18$^{th}$ July. From there we were going to fly to Moscow in the evening for a two-night stay. We were to fly back to the UK on Friday 20<sup>th</sup> July from Moscow on Aeroflot flight SU2241 to Edinburgh.

The trip began with much excitement. All students had arrived at Sheffield's Pond Street Bus Station with their parents, and packed lunches. Before we could get on the coach, the Sheffield Star newspaper turned up to take a group photo. We were a bit of an anomaly – a trip like this had not happened before with a group of students from some of Sheffield's state schools.

I certainly remember the Aeroflot flight from Gatwick. As soon as the plane took off, one of the light fittings above the aisle fell out! One of the air hostesses came to fix it. A little later, trays of food were brought out and this really was our first introduction to Soviet food. There were many varieties of pickled vegetables, including gherkins and peas. I can't remember what else was on the tray, but everyone was complaining about how disgusting it was!

**Leningrad**

The plane landed according to schedule, and we were taken by coach to the Hotel Karelia in Leningrad. This hotel was built in 1979 for the 1980 Olympics. It was a pretty non-descript block and about eighteen floors high. We were all assigned a room, which was shared with one other person. The view outside the window was also non-descript – identical blocks of concrete as far as the eye could see. I unpacked my suitcase and filled a glass of water from the tap. I added two water purifying tablets my mum had bought from *Boots* and waited for them to dissolve. According to the information leaflet we had been given at school, the tap water in Leningrad was not to be drunk because it contained harmful microorganisms. We were advised to use water purifying tablets if drinking tap water on our trip.

That evening, we all had dinner in the hotel restaurant. It was very basic, chicken, some other boiled meat, potatoes, and the ubiquitous pickles. We were given bottles of Soviet *Pepsi Cola* to drink. Our group stayed in the restaurant for some time, chatting about the day's events until the teachers told us to go to bed. We had a long day of sightseeing ahead of us the next day as well as a flight to catch to Donetsk the next evening. We all went to our rooms. It was difficult to get to sleep because of the white nights for which the northern hemisphere is known during the summer months.

The next day we spent sightseeing around Leningrad: The Peter and Paul Fortress, Rostral's Column, the exterior of the Hermitage Museum. In the evening we caught the flight to Donetsk after a last dinner at the hotel in Leningrad.

## Donetsk

I don't remember the journey to Donetsk, but I do remember how hot it was once we had landed at the airport. On our way to the hotel in the coach, we could see water vans spraying down the dusty streets. Being only fourteen at the time and abroad in the Soviet Union, water vans were kind of exotic. I certainly hadn't seen any in Sheffield!

We arrived at the hotel called the *Hotel Shakhtior*, which was named after the local football team. *Shakhtiory* are mines and Donetsk had plenty of them, just like South Yorkshire at that time. The hotel was situated near the Olympic and Donbass Arena stadiums. The architecture was typically Soviet with a conference and dining hall shaped like a flying saucer. Just before the 2012 Football Euros, it underwent reconstruction and was renamed *Hotel Shakhtar Plaza*. All members of our group were once again allocated hotel rooms where we dropped off our luggage and then we went for a late dinner in the flying saucer hall. We were going to visit a pioneer camp the next day, so we headed back up to our rooms straight after dinner. As we were making our way towards the lifts, I started to feel very queasy. The lift arrived and a few of us got in. The doors closed and the lift started to ascend to our floors. Suddenly, I violently vomited all over the lift floor. Everybody moved back against the lift walls to avoid being splattered. The doors opened and I made a run for my bathroom. My stomach hadn't quite finished. I was sick a few more times, and the Russian teacher from my school came to see how I was. She was probably hoping that I would be better by the morning. I was overcome by tiredness and went to bed. I woke up the next morning and managed to eat some breakfast before boarding the coach that was to take us to the pioneer camp. Unlike in Leningrad, we had two police escorts in Donetsk, one at the front leading the way and one bringing up the rear. We arrived at the pioneer camp with a welcome like no other. We were greeted by the whole camp around a flagpole, and given bread and salt, which is a typical welcoming ritual in this part of the world. We were divided in pairs and grouped with a Ukrainian pair who would be our hosts for the day. It was rather difficult to communicate with our Ukrainian friends because our Russian at that time was only basic phrasebook level and the pioneers didn't speak any English. I remember at the time I was undergoing orthodontic treatment and was wearing a brace to straighten my teeth. It was fixed onto my teeth with surgical cement and came complete with elastic bands to encourage my teeth to move into place. The pioneers had never seen anything like it and kept pointing to it. My phrasebook wasn't sufficient to explain what it was.

As for the rest of that day, well, it turned into a bit of a nightmare. After being paired up with the pioneers, my stomach turned queasy again. I started vomiting, not onto the floor, but into my handbag! I was escorted back to the coach by my Russian teacher who asked the police escorts to call an ambulance and take me to hospital. She came with me to interpret.

I spent most of the week in a Donetsk hospital and eventually recovered. I was very well looked after by a nurse called Vera and other medical staff who kept visiting me and sticking needles into my backside. I was given a room to myself, which had lovely houseplants and a very plush rug on top of a very highly polished parquet floor. I didn't know if the other rooms and wards were like this. As I recovered, I was fed black rye bread and some sort of cold pink drink, which I presumed was glucose because of its sweetness. My Russian teacher came to visit me a couple of times and asked if I needed anything. I requested my Russian phrasebook and some clean knickers from my suitcase at the hotel. Poor woman! Well, I was only fourteen after all.

The only other memory I have of the hospital was of the bathroom. It was situated down the corridor from my room. It was very basic, and you could smell it before you reached it. It was really bad! There was a white hand towel hanging on a peg by the wash basin, but it seemed as if this towel was for the entire hospital to use. It was filthy and had brown skid marks smeared all over it. I decided not to use it.

After a few days, I was discharged from the hospital and taken back to the hotel by my Russian teacher and another member of staff to join the rest of the students. We were leaving for Moscow the next day to do some sightseeing before our return to the UK.

**Moscow**

In Moscow, we stayed in the most luxurious abode I had ever seen in my life up to that point. It far surpassed the hotels in Leningrad and Donetsk. It was situated in one of the wedding-cake style Seven Sisters' buildings that had been built by Stalin. It was enormous. The hotel was located on the western bank of the Moscow River, and opposite the *Kazanskii Vokzal* (Kazan train station). Inside the foyer and in all public spaces were bronze statues and huge glistening chandeliers. Many famous people had apparently stayed there, and it was the location from which many spy novels had been set. It was rumoured that all the rooms were bugged. It was called *Gostinitsa Ukraina* (Hotel Ukraine). It still exists as a luxurious five-star hotel today, but nowadays it is called *The Radisson Collection Hotel Moscow*, after it was recently refurbished. It still has all the bronze statues and chandeliers and is absolutely stunning. There is a bar on the ground floor across the foyer as you walk in. Anybody can visit the bar, as I often used to when waiting for a train to Kazan later in life when I went to work and research in Russia. It was a far better option than waiting in the Kazan train station and being harassed by beggars for money every couple of minutes.

Among the memorable events that happened in Moscow was a trip to *Gosudarstvennyi universal'nyi magazin* or the State departmental store (GUM) on Red

Square. It had been called this since the 1917 Russian Revolution until the collapse of the Soviet Union and was then renamed to *Glavnyi universal'nyi magazin* (Main department store). It was built in 1893 and was the largest shopping mall across the Soviet Union. It was built on three levels, which were interconnected by ornate bridges. It ceased to be a shopping centre under Stalin and became an office building where members of the Politburo would work. After Stain's death it became a shopping mall once again. There were no shortages in GUM and citizens would queue for hours to buy hard-to-find goods. However, people could not just visit when they wanted – they were only allowed to shop on designated days according to where their surnames fell alphabetically.

During our trip there we wandered around looking at the shops, but it was not as extravagant as what it would become after the 1990s. It was a bit run down and reminded me of Sheffield markets. We found a badge store and bought some Lenin badges as souvenirs to take home.

Another shopping event was the *Berozhka* shop on some street in Moscow near our hotel. These shops were only open to high-ranking elites at this time, or foreigners with hard currency to spend. I don't think anybody from our group bought anything there.

I remember getting into a spot of bother in the Moscow metro. We were all given a green plastic jeton before we entered the palatial underground world. I didn't know why we had been given this at first, but discovered too late that it was the way to enter the metro. I just followed the person in front of me only to find myself trapped in a barrier gate with a transport policewoman blowing a whistle at me and then screaming loudly at me. I was so embarrassed. What had I done? Well, I hadn't realised that I should have inserted the jeton into the barrier in order for it to open. Oops! I survived.

We arrived back in Sheffield on Friday 20th July via Edinburgh. All our parents were waiting for us. I still wasn't sure what my illness had been, probably gastroenteritis, but I survived, as I did during many further adventures to what would become the post-Soviet space several years later.

# Part 2

# Transition to the Post-Soviet Space

**Chapter 2: The Transition to the Post-Soviet Period**

After seventy years of Communist rule and the events leading up to the failed coup in August 1991, the Soviet Union disintegrated. In its place, independent states and autonomous republics formed. The Baltic States, Ukraine, Belarus, Moldova, countries in Transcaucasia and the Central Asian Republics became fourteen independent countries and the Russian Soviet Federal Socialist Republic became the independent Russian Federation. The Russian Federation is governed by the central government in Moscow under the Russian Constitution and at the beginning of the post-Soviet period it was composed of eighty-three 'federal subjects'. These federal subjects consisted of twenty-one autonomous republics that had some degree of power, their own constitution, government, and president, but they remained politically situated within the Russian Federation (such as the Republics of Tatarstan and Bashkortostan). There were forty-six *oblasts*, each of which had a government representative and had less power than the autonomous republics. There were also *krais* and *okrugs* within the Federation plus Moscow and St Petersburg that were classed as federal cities and in 2014 *Sevastopol* in Crimea was also given the status of federal city.

What has been of particular interest to me regarding the collapse of the Soviet Union is the language situation across this vast geopolitical space. The official language of the Soviet Union was Russian, but before the formation of the Soviet Union, the Russian Empire, as this territory was previously named, was a vast multilingual and multi-ethnic territory; over one hundred and eighty languages were spoken. The people inhabiting the rural areas of this vast territory identified themselves in terms of kinship, language, and religion, not nationality[3].

When the Bolsheviks came to power after the Revolution in 1917, they were faced with the difficulty of having inherited such an ethnically diverse country. The Bolshevik government therefore fostered economic, political, and cultural policies to help the construction of the Soviet state[4].

As far as the economic policy was concerned, the countries of central Asia, Transcaucasia, Belarus, and many other territories of Russia were believed to be economically backwards, so a process of industrialisation began.

Cultural policies were concerned with the indigenisation of the population. This process of indigenisation was known as *korenizatsiia* and included linguistic developments such as a literacy campaign, the standardisation of the Russian language, non-Russian languages and writing systems for languages that did not have a written form. All national groups were encouraged to study their native language, and nobody was overtly pressured into studying Russian during this early period of communism[5]. However, the situation began to change during the 1930s when further steps were taken towards the construction of the Party's Soviet nationality through the assimilation of all peoples and the Russification of all languages.

Stalin's rule marked the second stage in the development of the nation state. In this stage Russian was to become the 'international lingua franca for economic, political and cultural cooperation' existing alongside separate nations and their separate languages[6].

Furthermore, the gerrymandering of nations was put into action to maximise intermingling and minimise the notion of the homelands[7]. Marxists had observed that people were more likely to assimilate if they were outside of their national homeland. *Korenizatsiia* was abandoned in 1934 and the move from a pluralistic language policy to an asymmetrical bilingual one was put in place as the second stage towards the unification of all peoples and assimilation of languages *(sblizhenie i sliianie narodov)*.

The main political goal of the Soviet government was the unification of all nationalities under a single Communist state based on assimilation of ethnic groups and not diversity. The purpose was to reach a higher stage of Communist development. Communication of the political agenda was of utmost importance for the Soviet government and communication would be eased if it went out in the multiplicity of languages spoken by the populace.

As the process of civilising societies continued over the Soviet period, so did the displacement of the national languages. Urbanisation and exposure to Russians had a large impact on the Russification of the Soviet non-Russian populations. If Russians migrated to rural areas, then there was more likely to be a weakening of rural traditions as well as more exposure to modern technology and mass communications. Therefore, if there were more Russians present demographically, then the Russification process would be more effective. Contemptuous attitudes towards non-Russian languages were bred, which was a sign of 'Russian autocratic chauvinism'. Disrespect towards the non-Russian languages was often shown in schools by Russian literacy teachers who apparently encouraged Russian students 'to leave native language classes and join their "own kind"'[8]. Such prejudice stemmed from family life and suspicions about religions, identity and different customs were passed down from generation to generation.

During the late Soviet period under Gorbachev's rule the promotion of Russian never ceased despite growing demands from the non-Russian nationalities. Russian was still the dominant language in the formation of a single socialist culture and of the new social and international community of the Soviet people[9]. The importance of Russian was cast in 'business-like tones'[10]. Bilingualism in 1989 amongst non-Russians was 48% and only 3.4% amongst Russians[11].

Under Gorbachev's *glasnost'* and *perestroika* policies the situation began to change. A resurgence of interest in the non-Russian languages started during the 1980s and under *glasnost'* the losses of these languages were allowed to be made public. Grass-roots movements formed to work towards the preservation of their cultures and to try to reverse asymmetrical bilingualism. In Ukraine and Belarus there was a particularly strong demand for two-way bilingualism[12]. In other republics, such as Georgia and the Baltics, many demonstrations took place against the domination of Russian and for the preservation of the non-Russian languages. Protests also took place over the low level of proficiency in non-Russian languages of Russians residing in these republics: non-Russian residents did not feel it was fair that they were bilingual or multilingual when Russians were monolingual[13]. The protests were about reinstating the titular languages as the official languages as well as the curtailment of Russian immigration[14]. English was readily accepted as a counterweight to the spread of Russian in many of the republics.

Criticisms were expressed about the marginalisation of non-Russian languages in schools and in everyday life as well as complaints regarding the preference of Russian over other languages on television[15]. Even applications for positions of employment were required to be completed in Russian in many of the central Asian republics[16]. The increasing domination of the Russian language had consequently led to the growth of national assertiveness. More opportunities arose for the non-Russian languages to serve as symbols for dissent[17]. The language issue was just one of the many contributing factors, which led to the collapse of the Soviet Union.

The perceived threat of Russian to the non-Russian languages resulted in the creation of legislation within the newly emerging republics that made their titular languages official and mandatory in all spheres for all citizens[18]. Estonia was one of the first to change its language policy in 1989, Turkmenistan in 1990 and the Russian language law of the Russian Federation was changed in 1991. These republics had a timeframe in which to shift their language policies to the titular language of the republic. The linguistic complaints of the nationalities became sentimental symbols, inciting new dynamics for ethnic unity[19]. These symbolic demands became instrumental demands as a consequence of Russian citizens residing in the territories of the Soviet Socialist Republics (SSR). In order to try to oust Russian citizens, laws were passed on the individual sovereignty of the non-Russian republics where separate trade delegations and currencies were established. In many cases this led to ethnic conflict: in order for Russians to survive in these ethnic republics, they had to become bilingual to be able to continue in employment[20].

At the end of the Soviet period the titular states and republics of the former Soviet Union began nation-building processes as a way to declare their identity after seventy years of cultural and linguistic suppression. Nation-building was concerned with de-Sovietisation processes, such as the replacement of Soviet political institutions with institutions of the titular nationality; the re-establishment of titular nations that included the codification of identity characteristics such as language and finally the discovery of the nation's past.

After the collapse of the Soviet Union the independent countries of the former Soviet state (such as in the Baltic States, where the titular language of each country was named as the official language) and the non-independent countries of the Russian Federation such as the autonomous republics all adopted either monolingual language policies or bilingual language policies that named Russian and the language of their titular nation as the official languages. The countries that had the most success in promoting the titular language after the collapse of the Soviet Union were the countries that included only the titular language in their language policies, such as the Baltic States (i.e. Latvian in Latvia, Lithuanian in Lithuania, and Estonian in Estonia). These countries quickly implemented monolingual language policies soon after the collapse of the Soviet Union as a means of establishing their identity.

It is against this backdrop that I studied, worked, and carried out research into the languages' situation of the post-Soviet space throughout my career. I was studying Russian and Soviet Studies at university in London when the USSR collapsed. I was due to go to Riga, the capital of Latvia in 1993 for my year of study abroad. Latvia had implemented a Latvian monolingual language policy to help re-establish its titular identity after Soviet repression. I was going there to improve my Russian. In fact, I didn't really know what was going on at that time, like so many others, both within and outside of the newly forming territories of the post-Soviet space.

**Part 2**

**Latvia**

**Chapter 3: Arrival**

In the early 1990s there were no direct flights from the UK to Riga, so I had to travel via Helsinki in Finland and catch the connecting flight to Riga the next morning. I spent the night in Helsinki airport, cautiously guarding my baggage and saxophone (which went everywhere with me) and trying to get some sleep. As you can imagine, it was quite difficult.

The next morning, I boarded the plane to Riga in trepidation of meeting the host family with whom I had been placed and having absolutely no idea who they were. The plane landed and everybody on board disembarked and made their way through customs and then to the arrival hall. There in front of me stood a couple holding up a placard with my name on it. The man was bearded, not very tall and well-wrapped up against the freezing January temperatures outside, as was the woman who had a kindly face and sparkly blue eyes. I made my way towards them and introduced myself. The man, who was called Vova (short for Vladimir), took my bags, although I kept a firm grip on my saxophone, and the woman was called Sveta (Svetlana) and led me outside to the taxi rank.

There was an awkward silence in the taxi on the way to Sveta and Vova's home. My Russian wasn't so good at the time, and they didn't speak any English – well, I was there to improve my Russian after all! The taxi passed through the centre of Riga and back out to the outskirts on the other side of the city. It was the height of winter and the landscape looked like somewhere out of a fairy-tale covered in deep snow. We drove past small, detached houses surrounded by frozen gardens. I was hoping the taxi would drop us off here. However, we continued and eventually came upon a brutalist style housing estate which seemed to go on and on.

It reminded me of the Kelvin, Park Hill, and Hyde Park flats in Sheffield from which residents would occasionally throw off TV sets and sometimes themselves. These flats had been built and completed in Sheffield in the 1960s; Park Hill was completed in 1961, Hyde Park in 1966 and Kelvin in 1967. The design of these estates had been inspired by the brutalist style and philosophy of the French architect Le Corbusier and were termed as streets in the sky because they had been designed with walkways and decks exposed to the elements. At the time, it was believed that these street designs would foster community life and were regarded as a social housing experiment. These estates had replaced back-to-back houses in which people had lived after the Second World War and were seen as a remedy to the housing crisis and squalid living conditions. Although the estates were popular places to live at the time and solved the problem of the housing crisis, inadequate maintenance, anti-social behaviour, poor noise insulation and poor safety and security caused the buildings and their reputations to decline. By the mid-1980s the estates were considered as failed social housing experiments by Sheffield City Council and the tenants were re-housed across the city. Some of the Hyde Park flats were renovated for the World Student Games in 1991 but were later pulled down. Park Hill underwent renovation after being designated as a grade two listed building, the largest listed building in Europe. Kelvin flats were demolished in 1995 and had become extremely run down and deemed unsafe. The complex was one of the most deprived areas in Sheffield during the mid-1980s due to the decline of the steel and coal industries as well as economic collapse in the city. It was during this demolition period in the early to mid-1990s that I found myself being driven through similar looking estates in Riga, but on a much bigger scale.

These brutalist housing estates only started to be constructed across the Soviet Union in the 1960s. They were also built as a social housing programme, much like in Britain at this time. However, in the early twentieth century, after the 1917 Revolution, shared living became a feature of Soviet life. Houses owned by the bourgeoisie were confiscated from them and divided up into shared accommodation known as *kommunalki*. Different families lived together in this type of accommodation and had to share cooking facilities and the bathroom. Each family was allowed thirty minutes to use the bathroom each day. Conditions were extremely cramped. When Khrushchev came to power after Stalin's death in 1953, he promised to end the housing crisis by building standardised blocks of flats. These flats were known as *Krushchevitsy* and built of concrete panels or bricks. They were five storeys high and were very small with no lifts. Despite this, every family had their own flat and was grateful for the privacy they had at that time. These five-storey blocks were uniformly built across the entire USSR; schools, cinemas and shops appeared in the local areas as well as communal gardens. All the needs of the individual were met. Although not all housing problems from the Stalin period were resolved, conditions did improve. When Brezhnev came to power (1964-1982), focus was on the construction of high-rise buildings. The blocks comprised nine to sixteen floors and were designed to be functional with all necessary amenities and infrastructure in the neighbourhood such as shops, health centres and schools housed on the first floor of the blocks. With mass industrialisation came urbanisation and new towns were built so that residents could easily reach their place of work. Housing estates were all built to the same standards including all cultural and service buildings in the localities. This accounts for why many blocks across the post-Soviet space all look the same.

I was hoping Sveta and Vova didn't live in one of these blocks, but the taxi pulled up outside the main door of one. I was feeling pretty petrified due to the social problems and crime that had been associated with such blocks of flats back home. However, as I discovered during my stay and subsequent visits to different parts of the post-Soviet space later on, I had nothing to worry about and just adapted.

We all got out of the taxi with my luggage and made our way inside towards the lift. The dark-grey concrete walls of the entrance were covered in graffiti and scruffy looking announcements were pinned to a communal noticeboard. There was a whiff of urine – hopefully from dogs. The lift arrived, its brown *Formica* doors rattled open, and we entered the small cabin. Sveta pressed for the seventh floor and the lift slowly took us up. We exited the lift and I found myself in a hallway not dissimilar to the one on the first floor, except there were four metal doors to different apartments and not as much graffiti. Sveta took out an enormous key and opened one of the doors. Behind the metal door was another maroon-coloured padded door, which had several locks. Finally, both doors were open revealing the hallway of their apartment. I entered, took off my coat and was presented with some *tapechki* (slippers) to wear. Sveta and Vova looked different without their winter wear. Both were dark and Sveta was taller than Vova. They put my luggage into what was to be my abode for six months and invited me to the kitchen for some tea and food. We had *kasha* (buckwheat) and salami, which was very welcome after my night in Helsinki airport. We chatted for some time about ourselves.

Sveta was originally from Belarus and spoke Belarusian, Russian, Latvian, and German. She was a German language teacher at one of the universities in Riga. In fact, later that morning she had to teach and couldn't stay around for long. Vova was originally from Moscow and he and his mother and sister had moved to Latvia during the Soviet period. Vova had been employed as an engineer but had recently become unemployed since the collapse of the USSR due to the newly implemented language policy which proclaimed Latvian as the official language of the country, and anybody wishing to work and claim Latvian citizenship had to pass a Latvian language competency exam. Vova didn't agree with the new regulations and was therefore unemployed.

Both Sveta and Vova had two children – Natasha who was thirteen and Andrei who was eleven. Both children were at school when I arrived, but when they came home, we introduced ourselves. It turned out that the room I had been given was Natasha's and she had been moved to share Andrei's room with him during my stay with them. Andrei was a whizz at chess, and he beat me every time we played. Natasha was an angry young teenager and was constantly arguing with her parents. In general, I got on well with the family (considering the horror stories I had heard about from the other students on my course at university).

## Chapter 4: Meat Cleaver Man

I was awoken one morning to the sound of a raucous male voice accompanied by an out-of-tune twangy guitar that sounded as if one or several of its strings were missing. It was extremely loud, and I wondered what was happening. I dragged myself out of bed – I didn't need to be at university until the afternoon and had planned to focus on writing my dissertation that morning. I wandered into the kitchen area to discover that no-one was around except for Vova. It wasn't him singing or playing the guitar, but he was obviously enjoying the music and didn't hear me come in. He was sitting at the small square table in the kitchen turning the handle of a meat cleaver, which was spewing out lumps of red meat for some sort of stew or goulash. He was singing along to the music, which was coming out of his and Sveta's bedroom. He stopped singing when he noticed me and got up to pour me some tea and make me breakfast. I asked what he was listening to, and he replied that it was a very famous Soviet singer called Vladimir Vysotsky. I had never heard of him at that time, but I learned more about his importance after Vova's introduction to him during that morning's meat cleavering.

Vysotsky was a symbol of dissent during the late Soviet period and called 'the voice of the heart of a nation' for the songs and poems he wrote in which he highlighted the suffering of the common people repressed under the Soviet regime. His music was restricted across the media under government censorship during the late Soviet period, so he went underground and distributed his music on the black market, as did many other musicians at this time. He had a huge fan base, but in 1980 his life was cut short by a heart attack as a result of drug addiction and alcohol abuse. His funeral overshadowed the 1980 Olympic games in Moscow, such was his popularity.

Vysotsky was not the only symbol of dissent present in popular culture during the 1980s. Another memorable rock band was *Kino*, which was led by Victor Tsoi as the group's main singer songwriter. The band were part of the Leningrad music scene in the 1980s, which was the heart of Soviet rock music. Tsoi's music career as well as his band's ended suddenly when Tsoi was killed in a car accident in 1990. Kino was particularly famous for the song *Khochu peremen* (I want changes), which became a protest anthem.

Other bands that the Leningrad rock scene brought to the fore included Aquarium, which still continues to perform to this very day. The band was formed in 1972 by Boris Grebenschikov. The band used to play in the kitchens of communal apartments and recorded their gigs on cassettes. Another example from the Leningrad rock scene was the musician Mike Naumenko and his band *Zoopark*. The band was popular in the Leningrad underground music scene at this time, but Mike Naumenko's life, as many other Soviet musicians during this period, was cut short due to drug addiction and depression. Naumenko and his band were immortalised as heroes of Soviet rock.

As *perestroika* and *glasnost* opened up new freedoms in Soviet society, western influences and Soviet rock music scene soon shifted the younger generation away from government allegiances. Rock music therefore created meaning and an outlet for Soviet youth who were tired of the customs of the older generations and the socialist environment of the time. Rock deviated from the norms of Soviet life and criticised the Soviet authorities, highlighting the plight of the common man and underprivileged groups in society.

Furthermore, as technology developed, shortwave radios allowed western rock music to infiltrate the air waves and influence music. These radios were unregulated by the Soviet authorities and so became popular and a means to learn about life on the other side of the iron curtain.

With the collapse of the USSR, this Soviet counterculture ended, although rock music was always considered as a symbol of hope and promise. Tsoi's anthem for changes came to the fore again during the 2020 election protests against the Lukashenko regime in Belarus. New rock bands, such as Pussy Riot, have also used music to protest against oppression and censorship under Putin's rule.

## Chapter 5: Richie Blackmore

Richie Blackmore was the founding member of the English hard rock music group Deep Purple in 1968. He was a singer songwriter and guitarist of the band and was known for his eccentric guitar riffs. Later he formed the heavy metal band Rainbow. Richie Blackmore was also the fifth member of Vova and Sveta's family. He was in fact their budgerigar and was adorned with bright blue and green plumage. He lived in a cage on the top of a shelf in the kitchen and was well looked after by all accounts, chirping away merrily to Vova's music. Vova told me that they had named him after Richie Blackmore because he (Vova that is) liked to listen to Deep Purple. Occasionally, he was let out of the cage to exercise his wings around the apartment, including the room in which I was staying.

One lunchtime Sveta called Natasha, Andrei, and me into the kitchen for lunch. I had been studying in the flat all morning and was pretty hungry. Just for once, we were not having a feast of potatoes and salami, but of macaroni and salami. The family often ate potatoes as their staple diet, as was usual during the Soviet period due to food shortages, and particularly during the collapse of the Soviet Union. It wasn't until we had sat down to eat at the kitchen table that I noticed Richie was out and about in the flat. I started to eat the pasta, which was very welcome, but just as I had started to eat, Richie flew into the kitchen, over the table and crapped into my pasta. It splattered everywhere! Bright green bird shit all over my macaroni. Natasha and Andrei were trying not to laugh as was Sveta while trying to catch the bird and put him back in his cage. I was also laughing but didn't want anything to eat after that (I didn't finish the pasta, by the way). Natasha and Andrei went into their shared room, and I could hear them laughing really loudly. Probably, Natasha thought it was my punishment for depriving her of her bedroom! After this, Richie wasn't allowed out during mealtimes.

## Chapter 6: Family Feast

It was a usual late Sunday morning in April in the family apartment – Andrei and Natasha were helping Sveta to clean up and were laying the family dining table in the front room. Vova was in the kitchen preparing food. I was busy reading and researching to make progress on my dissertation. The food smelt really nice, and I wondered what the occasion was. At about one o'clock I heard the doorbell ring and Sveta went to open it. It was Vova's sister Vera and her daughter Tanya who had been invited to Sunday lunch. I was introduced to them and learned that it was Tanya's twelfth birthday.

Vera and Tanya had brought flowers and apples to the festivities and put them in the kitchen. Tanya had severe special needs with cerebral palsy and was looked after full time by her mother, Vera. She attended a special needs school, but Vera said it wasn't helping her mental development. She kept asking me if I could find a place for her in a school in the UK where she had heard treatment for children with special needs was excellent. I had no idea where she had received her information, but I had no idea what to advise her. Often, severely disabled children of the Soviet Union would be sent to institutions by their parents who could then forget about them. This was usual practice in the Soviet period and was still continuing after the collapse of the USSR. The institutions would be situated in the countryside out of sight and mind, and well out of reach of the general public. Attitudes towards the disabled were shocking. However, Tanya was part of the family, and it was clear that she was loved by her family.

Just as Vera was asking me about special needs schools in the UK, Sveta called us all to the table – and what a spread there was! There were many plates of cold meats, cheeses, bowls of salad, sweets, and cakes as well as vodka and *compot* for the children.

Before starting the feast, it is necessary to explain what some of the food was on the table. Firstly, there was an *Olivier* salad, previously named *Stolichny salat* (table salad) during the Soviet period. This salad had first been invented by a chef named Lucien Olivier in Moscow in the mid-1800s. The salad originally comprised capers, black caviar, grouse, and crayfish, but during the 1930s the capers were no longer part of it, and it was difficult at that time to get hold of grouse. The salad was therefore reinvented and became *Stolichny salat*. Boiled meats, such as chicken or ham replaced the grouse, and peas were added along with carrots. In Moscow boloney sausage was used instead of boiled meats. Other ingredients that were eventually added were potatoes, eggs, pickles, and mayonnaise – loads of mayonnaise. After the collapse of the Soviet Union its name reverted back to *Olivier salat*. This was one of the dishes of the day.

*Compot* is a stewed fruit drink from which fruits are collected by families during the autumn and left to ferment in water with sugar and lemon juice. It was very sweet and refreshing. Another dish on the table was a plate of chicken cutlets. Cutlets can be made from any type of meat and are made by covering them in breadcrumbs and frying them. There were also freshly made *pirozhki* (little pies) that were filled with both cabbage and onions. There was a plate of bright red tomatoes and another of gherkins to name but a few. We sat down at the table and began with a vodka toast to the birthday girl. She didn't drink any vodka! After this Sveta passed around the table a plate of white sweets, which I was told was used to take the bitter taste of the vodka away. I took a piece and put it in my mouth. Instead of a sweet taste, all I could taste was lard. My whole mouth became invaded with the full greasy fat of whatever it was. It was disgusting and I immediately felt sick. I simply could not hide the horror of the flavour and texture of this delicacy through the expression on my face. Sveta passed over the plate of tomatoes for me to take one and get rid of the greasy lard in my mouth. I gratefully took a tomato and bit into it expecting it to be a very ripe flavoursome tomato to release me from the fat and cleanse my mouth. Unfortunately, the tomato was pickled, which I had never tasted nor heard of up to that point in my life. There are no actual words to describe the taste apart from it was disgusting. I didn't know which was worse – the greasy lard or the tomato. By now everyone was watching me to see if the tomato had gone down well – it hadn't and in fact I didn't swallow any. This time Sveta passed me a tin of something potent to wash it all down with. It was like a Bacardi and coke, but it did the trick and soon I was merrily chatting away to Vera and Tanya, slowly getting pickled myself. Vera was obviously wearing a blond wig, which by the end of the afternoon had slipped forward onto her forehead, making her look like Chewbacca from Star Wars. The afternoon passed quickly but I can't remember what else I ate (if anything) due to the tinned alcohol on offer in between toasts of vodka. I did discover what the lard was though. It was called *salo* and was made from pig fat, salt, and black pepper. It was a popular *zakuski* (appetizer) to have with vodka. I have never eaten it since nor will I ever again and will always be cautious when offered white sweeties. I will never eat pickled tomatoes again either. Whenever I was invited to somebody's home in the post-Soviet space for food in the future, I always remembered the experience with the family in Latvia to this very day.

**Part 3**

**The Closed Administrative Territories of the Soviet Union**

After the Second World War, many cities were built across the Soviet Union that were hidden not only from the 'so-called' enemies outside of the Soviet Union (the west, the US), but also from the inhabitants of the Soviet Union itself. The cities were mainly built by prisoners from the Gulag labour camps and were surrounded by barbed wire fences and guards. Some of these cities were classified as science cities (*naukogorodoki*) and others as academic cities (*academgorodoki*). Some of these cities developed military equipment, others nuclear and atomic energy, and spacecraft. Collectively, these cities were known as 'closed administrative territories' (*zakrytye administativno-territorial'nye obrazovaniia* or ZATO). Many of these cities did not have proper names – they were identified by a label and a postal code, and they did not even feature on maps until 1993 when they were declassified.

Permission had to be obtained from the authorities to exit and enter these cities and relatives of the residents living there had to acquire a special pass to enter. They were only allowed to stay for a short time and certainly not overnight. The residents were sworn to secrecy about their activities but were highly rewarded with a higher standard of living than in the rest of the country, including a high standard of health care, better quality food, guaranteed employment, and their own private apartments. To compensate for being culturally cut off from the rest of the country, Houses of Culture were built in which specially invited musicians performed, including rock groups. Of course, they were sworn to secrecy. Fashion shows, festivals, discotheques, and other such events were put on to keep the boredom of living in a closed city at bay.

After the collapse of the Soviet Union, some of these cities became declassified and changed their labels to proper city names. For example, *Arzamas-16* became *Sarov*, *Chelyabinsk-16* became *Ozersk*. If you happen to take a long train journey through the post-Soviet space these days, you will often pass train stations in the middle of nowhere, which are labelled as just the number of kilometres away they are situated from Moscow (i.e. *395km*). There still exist many closed territories across the post-Soviet space. When these closed cities appeared on maps from 1993 onwards, the rest of the world was afraid of what had been happening and of the knowledge of the scientists and academics working in these cities pertaining to atomic and nuclear power. As relations between the east and west slowly thawed at the beginning of the Soviet period, scientific, academic, and cultural bridges were built to improve relations and to share knowledge.

The following two chapters are about two of these closed cities in which I went to live and work.

## Chapter 7: Kaliningrad aka Korolev - The Soviet Space Flight Control Centre

In 1994 after I had graduated, I successfully completed a Teaching English as a Foreign Language course (TEFL) and went to Russia to teach in an English language school set up by my university Russian teacher in London and a husband-and-wife team who were from and living in Russia. They were called Vera and Dima (the other teachers and I called them VD as a nickname). They were utterly obnoxious and had only just set up their language school in Kaliningrad, a closed science city in the Moscow region. It was also called *Star City*.

Kaliningrad was known for its Soviet Space Flight Control Centre, which had been established in the city in the mid-1970s. The city itself existed long before it became known as a centre for scientific space research. Its earliest roots can be traced back to the twelfth century when it was just a small village where local Slavs lived. In the seventeenth century, as the village grew, the first cloth and wool manufacturers in Russia were established on this territory. By the end of the nineteenth and beginning of the twentieth centuries, the expanding village and industry in the area had become a town and was named Kaliningrad in 1938. With the threat from Germany and the First World War, the Petrograd Ammunitions Factory was moved to Kaliningrad for safety. Other factories were established in Kaliningrad during the 1930s. The two main ones were firstly, the *Kurchevskii Zavod*, which developed dynamic non-recoil projectile weapons, and the *Chizhevskii Zavod*, which developed long distance airplanes. Other factories, such as the *Grabina Zavod* manufactured tanks and cannons.

In 1946 the *OKB-1* (construction bureau) was founded by Sergei Korolev and was later renamed as *RKK Energia,* the Russian Space Rocket Corporation. It was known as one of the leading businesses for the Russian space research and rocket industry. Korolev was the creator of the Soviet space rocket as well as a key figure in space exploration programmes, including the launch of the first satellite. He was responsible for putting the first cosmonaut in space – Yuri Gagarin.

Over time, Kaliningrad expanded even further, and many former villages were incorporated into the town's territory, including the villages of Kostino, Pervomaiskii and Bolshevo. Many of these villages had been dwarfed by the construction of *Krushchevitsy* five-storey blocks during the 1950s, then by huge brutalist blocks to house the expanding population from the 1960s onwards.

In 1996 Kaliningrad was renamed Korolev (as many former Soviet towns and cities were renamed after the collapse of the USSR) in honour of the great scientist. Many academics and scientists came to work in the town, which was a closed town at the time I was there. Kaliningrad (as it was still named while I was there) also had the highest mortality rates of HIV in the whole of the Russian Federation due to drug abuse and needle sharing.

Many of the students who we taught in the language school were engineers, military workers, or university teachers. One of the English teachers had a student called Alexei, who was quite high ranking in the military and worked at the Kaliningrad Space Flight Control Centre. He invited all the teachers from the language school along with a couple of students to attend the launch of the Soyuz spacecraft from the Kaliningrad Space Flight Control Centre one Saturday morning in March 1995. The spacecraft was going to launch from Bakanur in Kazakhstan. I was invited to act as interpreter. Well, I couldn't refuse, could I?!

Fortunately, I had had some experience of space terminology through translation practice exercises at university.

Alexei met us outside the gates of the Soviet Space Flight Control Centre, which was heavily guarded. We were ushered into the building and had to go through strict security checks. Once these were passed, we were all issued with visitor passes and shown the ubiquitous cloakroom where we had to leave our coats and bags. Actually, this cloakroom was not the same as all others in Russia because the numbered plastic counters handed over to us in exchange for our belongings were shaped like planets. It was very Star Trek! From here we were led through some corridors and then into a massive hall where the mission control room was situated. We were in awe of the hall and could not quite believe we were there. At one end of the hall, there was a huge screen with a map of the world on it. Around the main screen were smaller screens each of which, we were told, focused on a particular part of the mission in more detail to check the functioning of different parts of the spacecraft and the mission itself. The whole hall was filled with rows upon rows of desks joined together and with high-tech computers on them. Behind the majority of the computers mission controllers were sat preparing for the spacecraft launch.

We were taken to a special viewing platform towards the back of the hall. From here we had an excellent view of what was happening. There was a member of staff acting as our guide who would be explaining to us what was going to happen during the flight, and I was in full interpreter mode. Suddenly, the countdown began, and we stood nervously watching the large screen. The Soyuz spacecraft took off from Bakanur, and there was a huge round of applause. We did not actually see the spacecraft (rather disappointing, I might add), but we saw a red dot on the map, which represented the spacecraft getting higher and higher above the Earth's orbit. We could see the astronauts inside the spacecraft on the mission controllers' screens. They were following flight instructions.

We were then told about the Soviet Space Flight Control Centre in more detail. According to our guide, the centre could control both Earth satellites and interplanetary probes such as the *Mir* orbital complex, the *Buran* shuttle system, the *Soyuz TM* and *Progress* spacecraft, the *Kvant* astrophysical module and the *Salyut 7* orbital station, as well as the *Vega* and *Phobos* unmanned interplanetary stations. Spacecrafts for tasks relating to the national economy and science were also designed at the centre. It was here where ballistic, navigation, telemetric, command and data support of space missions were carried out. It also had powerful communications and data gathering systems, high speed computers (which did not really exist for the outside world at that time) and high-tech information display systems.

Another mission of the Soviet Space Flight Control Centre was the continued search for co-operation with experts and scientific organisations all over the world to foster peaceful space exploration and to use space achievements for the benefit of humanity. Many international scientists and experts came to work at the centre during international missions.

After about an hour, the guide left us and Alexei, the student, led us to another part of the building. He took us into an archive where photos of all astronauts who had participated in various missions were placed on the walls as heroes of the country. We were also shown models of spacecraft and old computing systems, spacesuits, and the type of food that the astronauts took with them on missions. Most of the food was puréed and put into tubes or special airtight trays. It did not look very appetizing at all. We were all given posters of the Soviet Space Flight Control Centre as souvenirs, but I doubt that any of us would ever forget that opportunity we had that day - it was phenomenal.

I have seen that since our visit in 1995 and since the city of Kaliningrad was renamed Korulev in 1996, the Soviet Space Flight Centre archives have been turned into a museum and anybody can go and visit. I might go back one day, if the situation allows...

*Figure 1: Poster from Soviet Space Flight Control Centre*

## Chapter 8: The Great Escape - from Dubna

A few days after I had arrived in Russia to teach in Kaliningrad, Vera and Dima informed me that the very next morning I would be taken to another town to work in a new English language school they had just set up. A flat had been arranged for my accommodation and I was to start testing students to assess their levels of English language proficiency as soon as I got off the train. The town was called Dubna, and I had no choice in the matter. Vera and Dima came to collect me and my luggage at four the next morning to catch the train from *Savelovskii vokzal* (the train station) in Moscow. I was a bit miffed that I had been deprived of a chance to go and see Red Square while passing through.

Once we had arrived at *Savelovskii vokzal,* VD bought the tickets and led me to the platform. The train was already there, and passengers were loading up shopping trolleys of potatoes and pickles onto it. The train itself was called the *Express* and was blue instead of the usual murky green of Russian railways. I was informed that it had been the only express train in existence during the Soviet period and it was because of the research that was carried out in Dubna that it was granted its very own express train. Actually, there was nothing very express about the train since the journey took just under four hours to cover 125 kilometres.

Dubna was another science satellite city that was closed to outsiders. It was the centre of nuclear research and had a nuclear reactor – no need to worry there then! Dubna had been established for one reason – the Soviet Union needed nuclear power and a testing centre to develop knowledge about elements and particles. While housing was being built for scientists, the first experimental accelerators were developed in 1949. It was only named Dubna in 1956 and given status as a town at this time. Prior to this, it didn't have a name and the area where these scientific buildings and scientist accommodation was being built was made up of a conglomeration of local villages and hamlets, such as Ivankovo. The town was built by forced labour from nearby prison camps.

Dubna is situated on the river Volga and Moscow canal, whose construction was completed in 1937. Many villages and settlements were flooded as a result of this canal construction. It is not far from the Ivankovo reservoir, formed by a hydroelectric dam and also built in the 1930s. The town is situated in a deeply forested area with many parklands. It was built here due to the geographical location near the hydro-electrical station because there would be less danger from earth tremors and fluctuations. The location was also far from Moscow and very remote, consequently, there would be less distractions for the scientists.

The year 1956 was a turning point for the town when the Joint Institute for Nuclear Research was founded, and the town became one of the largest scientific centres in the world. The town was officially named Dubna and scientists from many socialist countries visited the nuclear research institute[21]. Analogically therefore, it was the equivalent of the Swiss CERN of the time.

So, what was I doing there? Well, I taught there for a few months until I decided to escape, which was no mean feat, considering that I managed to get a new teaching job in Moscow, but was still registered on the work permit and visa from Vera and Dima. How did I get to Moscow then? Well, if I go back to the beginning from when I arrived in Dubna, I was taken to an impromptu English language testing centre not far from Dubna's main train station immediately after stepping off the train. Students were organised according to levels of proficiency, and I was to teach them in a classroom of a primary school from three in the afternoon to nine o'clock every weekday evening. I was given a flat, which belonged to the mother of the Dubna English language school's co-ordinator called Irina. The flat was on the nineth floor of an apartment block situated in the sticks opposite a large forest. I was shown where the shops were (two of them) and where to catch the bus to the school. That was it! I was left on my own completely, or so I thought. In fact, I had been designated chaperones to guide me around and make sure I didn't get lost (or escape). They were both students in my English classes. One was called Lena and worked at the Joint Institute for Nuclear Research, and the other was called Vadim who had suffered from mental health issues after carrying out his compulsory military service. He didn't live far from me and used to drop by with bottles of cognac and vodka now and again. He was working in a nursery in the local area. I also remember that he had made his own winter coat, which was impressive.

The monthly salary I received at the school was US $30, a mere pittance. I couldn't do anything with it except buy a few Bush legs (chicken legs donated by George Bush senior to help with the post-Soviet transition presumably) at the local outdoor market. After the first month, I decided to teach the students privately from the flat I had been given. This way I would earn more money. However, this didn't go down well with Vera and Dima who had been informed of my movements by Irina! Paradoxically, Irina also came to the flat and got free English lessons out of me.

One evening in late November 1994, my chaperones invited me to a jazz festival in the Dubna House of Culture. It was very fortuitous for me because I made the acquaintance of two other English teachers who were at the festival and who were working at Dubna University through a company called *Language Link*. Lena introduced me to them because she worked part time in Dubna University as an administrator (as well as her job at the research institute). After having a good chat with the two teachers about what we were all doing in Dubna, they gave me the phone number of their boss in Moscow who I phoned the next day to ask for a new job. I was invited to Moscow for an interview (although I had to take the express train without being discovered by Irina who lived in a block opposite the train station). I got the job, and a date was set for me to begin. The plan was that I would be met at *Savelovskii vokzal* (the train station) in Moscow by Tolya, the *Language Link* driver. The director of *Language Link* had given me money for the train ticket to Moscow and we agreed to keep in touch by phone until the day of escape.

I continued teaching in the flat until the day of my departure. I hadn't told anybody, especially not Irina, I was leaving and had already bought my train ticket. I packed my bags, hiding them in the wardrobe so that nobody would be suspicious while I was teaching. The next morning, I locked up, put the key in the letter box, set off with my luggage and caught the bus to the station.

A fresh layer of snow had fallen overnight so it was a bit of a struggle up to the train platform. When I arrived, there was a notice on the ticket office window, which informed passengers that trains to Moscow had been cancelled until later in the day. I couldn't believe it! I didn't know what to do. I couldn't go back to the flat and I couldn't drag my luggage anywhere to wait for the later train. I couldn't even phone the language school in Moscow to tell them I would be late (mobile phones didn't exist back then). Then, the worst thing that could happen actually happened. Irina had spotted me on the platform from her window and came out of her building over to me. She took me to her apartment with my luggage and asked what I was doing. I told her! I asked if I could use her phone and she at least let me do this. She was very upset but said I could wait in her apartment until the later train. It was very awkward. I really thought that I would either be locked in her apartment, kidnapped by some of her husband's dodgy friends, or even murdered on the way to the train station later.

Actually, none of this happened and I made my way safely to the train later that afternoon. Tolya was waiting for me in Moscow and drove me to my new abode in Moscow. I started teaching the following week in the *Language Link* school, which was situated in an old block of flats on *Ulitsa Marx-Engels* (Marx-Engels Street) ten minutes' walk away from Red Square. So, I finally got to see it!

It wasn't the end of my problems with Vera and Dima though because I was registered to work for them and bureaucracy in Russia was notoriously difficult at that time (and still is). The head of *Language Link* had to meet them and pay them a bribe in order to make them leave me alone. Even when I left Moscow for a break to return to the UK for a month, the head of *Language*

*Link* had to pay another bribe to the airport officials because my original visa terms had run out. I had to re-apply for another visa back in the UK to get back to Moscow for the next academic year. I stayed in Moscow for two years before moving on to other countries to work. I had enjoyed my time there, especially the second year without so many of the issues I'd faced previously.

# Part 4

# The Republic of Tatarstan

Tatarstan is a multi-ethnic autonomous republic, which is politically situated within the Russian Federation. Kazan is the capital city and is situated at the convergence of the Kama and Volga rivers approximately eight hundred kilometres east of Moscow. Tatarstan is situated on the west side of the Ural Mountains and on the eastern edge of the European part of the Russian Federation[22]. It shares its borders with the republics of Mari El, Udmurtia, Bashkortostan and the *oblasts* of Samara, Kirov, Orenburg and Ulyanovsk. Tatarstan is a non-Russian republic, and both the Russian-Orthodox and Sunni Muslim religions are practised. The Tatar language is a western Turkic-Altaic language and is the result of complex linguistic contact from Kipchak Turkic, Volga Bulgar, Volga Finnic and Mongolic[23]. It is closely related to the Bashkir language[24].

According to the 2010 all-population census results[25], 3.7 million people reside in Tatarstan of which 53.2% are Tatars, 39.7% Russians, 3.1% Chuvash and 4% is made up of other nationalities, such as Udmurts, Kriashens, Bashkirs, Bulgars and Azeris. Tatars and Russians have coexisted with each other over many centuries. As a result of this coexistence, two types of bilingualism have developed: Tatar-Russian, which refers to the language behaviour of Tatars and Russian-Tatar, which refers to the language behaviour of Russians[26]. However, bilingualism in Tatarstan is considered to be asymmetrical due to the developments and dominance of the Russian language during the Soviet period. Asymmetrical bilingualism means that Russians are monolingual in Russian only whilst non-Russians are bilingual in their native language and Russian. In Tatarstan Russians speak Russian and Tatars may speak both Tatar and Russian. I was going there to research how effective the Tatar language policy had been in promoting the spread of Tatar language use by analysing Russians' and Tatars' Tatar language proficiency levels in universities across Kazan. I had a huge mountain to climb as I didn't know anybody who had been there and nobody from my university had been there either. I had to cross so many hurdles and the visa process was one of the first.

## Chapter 9: Visa Registration in Kazan

Visa registration is a complicated process in Russia. It doesn't just start with deciding which type of visa is required such as a single entry, multi-entry tourist, business visa, visa for study or visas to visit friends only. If you get the wrong visa, you could be deported, or worse still, end up in a Russian prison (definitely not recommended!). To get a visa you will also need an invitation either from a Russian registered institution such as a tourist company, university, business, or a letter from a friend.

For my first trip to Russia in over ten years to carry out data collection for my PhD I chose the single-entry tourist visa with an invitation to visit a friend. The 'friend' was actually a Russian-Tatar couple living in Sheffield who were training to be doctors at the University of Sheffield. Both had trained as doctors in Russia and had worked in the Accident and Emergency department in one of Kazan's hospitals. They were called Natalia and Mekhmet and had a five-year old daughter who attended a Saturday Russian school/nursery in a church hall in Sheffield. I had been given their contact details via a colleague at the university with the hope that they could help me with accommodation in Kazan.

I knew nobody else in Kazan at that time, except for a girl I had met online when I had signed up to a Skype conversation exchange to practise my Russian. I hadn't spoken it for a few years, not since when I had briefly worked as a public services interpreter in Sheffield. She was from Kazan, called Nastya, and was an IT consultant working for a company in Kazan. She needed to practise her English for work purposes. We came to an arrangement that we would meet online every week on a Sunday evening and alternate our languages on a weekly basis. Just before I went to Kazan, Nastya gave me her phone number and told me to contact her once I had arrived.

During a conference I had attended earlier in 2010, I had been given the name of an academic who worked in the Russian department in Kazan State University. I had written to this contact, but she had been slow to reply. She later helped me to distribute surveys at the university, although she was extremely biased about my research. I was later given another random contact by Natalia who worked in the social science faculty in the same university in Kazan. Apparently, Natalia went to school with this contact and had kept in touch with her on Facebook. I wrote to her, and she gave me her phone number so I could contact her once I was in Kazan.

Natalia and Mekhmet had an apartment in Kazan and said I could rent it from them during the month I was going to be there. I explained to them that I would need help registering my visa when I arrived within the first three days of my arrival. This seemed a simple enough process as I found out I could do this at the main post office in Kazan. Natalia said her mother could help me and even organised her mother, stepfather, and sister to meet me at the airport and take me to their apartment. Everything was going to plan…

I set off on 3rd October 2010 with my luggage full of 200 surveys, a few clothes, and my laptop, which weighed a tonne! I was full of trepidation, flying to a random city somewhere in the outback of Russia and knowing nobody. I was worried that Natalia had set me up and nobody would meet me at the airport, and just maybe the apartment didn't really exist. I had Natalia's e-mail address, but what if I couldn't connect to the Internet?! I was struggling badly with my hormones at the time and experiencing extremely heavy flooding and insomnia due the wrong type of HRT for menopause management. I was a mess!

The flight was overnight and stopped off in Frankfurt where I had to transit to my connecting flight to Kazan. This flight stopped off in Samara before finally landing in Kazan at 6am. The plane from Frankfurt to Kazan was full, but when it stopped off in Samara, all but three people, including myself, disembarked. Why was nobody else going to Kazan? What was the problem? The plane took off and I was seriously beginning to panic. The air hostesses gave me all the leftover chocolate bars they had, which I was very grateful for, in case I was stranded in Kazan with nowhere to go.

The plane landed on time, and I disembarked, sailed through customs, and much to my relief there was a sign with my name on it. I approached who I presumed was Natalia's mother, called Liudmila, her husband Sergei and the sister, whose name I forget and who I only met that once. Sergei took my luggage to the car, and we made our way through the busy rush hour traffic of Kazan. My first impressions of the city were not favourable. The blocks of flats look shabby as if they needed renovation. I also noticed that the tram tracks looked old, rusty, and as if they had all buckled. This wasn't the case though because equally shabby red trams were running along the tracks, albeit very slowly. Sergei pulled in outside a hospital and Natalia's sister got out. She hadn't spoken a word to me at all. Perhaps it was too early in the day for a conversation with a foreigner (or she was just a miserable bitch!). Apparently, the whole family worked in the hospital except Sergei, who I later found out was unemployed.

We finally arrived at the apartment building on Dzerzhinsky Street. I was shocked. The whole building was covered in large cracks from the guttering to the floor. The road and driveway to the entrance of the building was a mud track. The surrounding area revealed many broken buildings with weeds growing out of cracks, and some fly tipping had evidently been going on.

*Figure 2: Entrance to my flat*

Sergei helped me out of the car along with Liudmila, and they escorted me to an outer door of the building, which was made of sheet metal and had gone rusty. We entered the building, which was only marginally better than the outside, and ascended the stairs to the third floor. Just as my previous experiences in Russia, Liudmila pulled out a huge key and opened the heavy iron door. Behind this door was a huge, padded door which led into the apartment. Sergei put my luggage down in the hallway and Liudmila showed me around the apartment. The first door on the right-hand side was the toilet and the room next to it, the bathroom. Down the corridor was the kitchen, with cooker, fridge and much to my delight, a washing machine. I was so relieved! I had had visions of me having to wash my clothes by hand in the bath, as I had done countless times while working in Russia and eastern Europe. Sergei followed us into the kitchen and wrote down his phone number on a piece of paper in case of any eventualities. They said the apartment was in the centre of Kazan, so I was close to shops and all amenities. I asked if they could register me within the next two days. They just looked at me blankly as if I was a babbling foreigner who didn't know anything about Russia. On that note they both departed leaving me on my own with the possibility of arrest for not registering my visa at that address. I also had no phone, no means of communication, nor a map of Kazan. I had 200 surveys in my suitcase and a few clothes. I was well and truly stuffed!

So, what did I do? Well, I put my pragmatic head on as I've learned is necessary in these kinds of situations. I decided to look in the kitchen cupboards and found some tea bags. I also found some dried macaroni, *kasha* (buckwheat), flour, the usual Russian kitchen cupboard fare. The fridge was more interesting. It was choc-a-block full of medicines and weird-looking cultures growing in large glass jars. There was also a carton of milk and some cheese, which Sergei and Liudmila had thoughtfully left for me. I suppose I could have bribed people on the street to answer my surveys with these medicines if necessary. After some much-needed tea, I decided to look around the apartment. It was surprisingly large, but gloomy. There were two rooms – one bedroom and a living room, which had a TV. It worked! There was also a radio, and tucked away in a corner on a small cabinet was a phone! How fortunate! I picked up the receiver expecting it to be dead, but there was a tone. Phew! At least I could get in touch with the three contacts I had. It seemed a little early to contact the people from the university, so I decided to go exploring the local area. On one side of the apartment through the window was a park. There was no grass, but plenty of mud. It looked like there was a kind of children's playground, with climbing frames that had gone rusty and plenty of peeling paint. There was what I presumed to be swings, but without seats. I discovered the next day that the park was called *Park chernogo ozera* (Black Lake Park). I don't know where that name came from because there was no lake to be seen.

*Figure 3: Park Chernogo Ozera*

On the other side of the apartment there was a door to the balcony. I opened it and decided not to step out onto it because it didn't look firmly attached to the outside wall. Looking across at the view, I could see some very old buildings that once upon a time would have been very grand. The blocks were green in colour, though extremely faded and rundown. The cracks in the walls were so wide that it looked as if the whole block would crumble at any moment. People actually lived there as well.

*Figure 4: A view of the local neighbourhood*

I decided to start exploring the street which ran parallel to Dzerzhinsky Street. This street was called Kremlovskaya Street and led directly to the Kazan Kremlin. I decided to go in the opposite direction to the Kremlin to find out if there were any supermarkets or mobile phone shops nearby. Tourism could wait until later! This street was quite wide and looked as if many of the buildings had had a recent fresh coat of paint. There were no shops as such, just government office buildings. There were not many people or traffic around either. Eventually, I came across a very palatial looking building, which was painted white and was fronted by large columns. It was Kazan State University! At least I had found the building where I could arrange to meet my two university contacts. That was a definite result on my first day. I continued walking down Kremlovskaya, which turned a corner to lead down a hill to a busier looking area. Perhaps this was the centre?

I arrived at the crossroads of the main street of Kazan called Baumanskaya Street. It was pedestrianised and shops lined both sides of the street. It ran parallel to Kremlovskaya Street and eventually led to the Kremlin complex. It looked interesting and I decided to have a walk along it to see what was on offer. There were very few people, but bloody hell, it was so noisy! Each shop had a loudspeaker attached to its outside wall and was blaring loud pop music from a radio station or something or other. Each shop played a different song, or radio station and it was really difficult to differentiate which tune was coming from which shop. What a cacophony of sound! It was awful, and I had had very little sleep. However, as I walked on a bit further, I came across a mobile phone shop. I decided to go in and buy a phone and SIM card. I was really making progress on my first day, or so I thought...

There was a young lad behind the shop counter, and he greeted me when I entered the shop. I said I needed a phone and a pay-as-you-go SIM. He showed me many models and asked what kind of SIM I wanted. He also asked me where I was from, what I was doing in Kazan, and if I liked The Beatles. I could tell I was in a small provincial town in the middle of Russia! Anyway, I finally bought what I needed. I was in the land of the living again! Well almost – I now needed an Internet connection and didn't know how to go about getting this. At least I could phone my contacts and get their advice. I asked the shop assistant where the nearest supermarket was, and he pointed out the shopping centre called *Koltso* at the other end of the street. I thanked him and went on my way. I was really hungry by this point and needed something to eat desperately before I collapsed in a heap on the pavement in the middle of Baumanskaya.

I arrived at the *Koltso* shopping mall via a dubious underpass at the end of Baumanskaya Street, where babushkas were selling huge knickers on small wooden tables next to kiosks selling either expensive silver jewellery or flowers. *Koltso* shopping mall was a five-storey building with shops on the lower floors and restaurants on the top. I wandered around the ground floor looking for a supermarket. I found fashion shops, shoe shops, cosmetics shops, but no supermarket. I took the escalator down to the lower ground floor and had a quick look round. Again, many more useless shops, as well as a gun shop! Guns were on display like toys in counters as well as ammunition. I'd never seen anything like this in Meadowhall, Sheffield. As I walked around the corner, I saw the supermarket. At last! I was so hungry – but not for long! As I entered the supermarket, I noticed just inside the entrance a huge pile of rotten apples in what appeared to be a replica field surrounded by low wooden fences. The stench was foul. I don't know how long the apples had been there, but they were probably past the best-before date. I don't think they would have made good cider either. I would recommend anybody wanting to go on a diet to go there! I lost my appetite.

I made my way past the mound of rotten apples. Were people seriously buying these? I wandered around the aisles of the supermarket and collected a few provisions to see me through the next couple of days: kefir, tvorog, which is a kind of compacted curd cheese, black rye bread and smoked hard cheese. In other words, all the products I used to buy when I worked in Moscow all those years ago. I paid, made my way out of the supermarket, the shopping mall and back to the apartment for a feast. It wasn't far and my first initial trip around the area had seemed more daunting than it actually was.

Once I had arrived back at the apartment and had eaten, I began to feel much better. I decided to make some calls. The first was to the academic called Nina in the Russian language faculty of the university. She was very pleasant and asked if my arrival had been OK and if I needed anything. I didn't, but we agreed to meet the next morning at the entrance of Kazan State University. I then called Gulnaz, Natalia's Facebook friend, and arranged to meet her at the university entrance later on the same day. Next, I called Nastya who wanted to meet me that very day after she had finished work at 6pm. We agreed to meet outside the "Rotten Apple Supermarket" because I didn't know anywhere else. I finally called Liudmila and Sergei to let them know my phone number and to ask them to register me tomorrow at some point. Again, they didn't know what I was going on about, so I decided that someone else would need to explain to them what I needed on my behalf. If only I had had an Internet connection, I could have emailed Natalia in Sheffield tell her how serious it would be for both her parents and me if I wasn't registered within three days of arrival. There was nothing more I could do that day, so I decided to go for another walk in the opposite direction towards the Kazan Kremlin. On the way, I discovered a tourist information office and got a map of Kazan. I was feeling quite relieved that I had achieved so much in one day and I was looking forward to meeting Nastya later.

Nastya and I met up at 6pm as arranged, and we went for some food in a sushi bar on the top floor of *Koltso*. I was very glad to have met her in person and she asked if she could help me with anything. I asked her about Internet access, and she took me to an IT shop in the shopping mall and got me a dongle to use for my laptop. What a relief! She walked me back to the apartment and suggested we meet up again in a few days or at the weekend when she could give me a proper tour of Kazan.

That evening, I connected to the Internet and emailed Natalia to explain that her relatives needed to register me or there would be problems for her mother, since she was the registered owner of the flat. Apparently, she would be liable for a huge fine if she didn't register me within three days of arrival. After this, I needed to prepare myself for meeting Nina from the Russian department the next morning to explain that I needed to distribute my surveys in the university and interview staff and students if possible.

I watched a bit of TV to wind down. All the news items were about plane crashes that had happened recently across the post-Soviet space and road accidents that had happened in Kazan. One item was particularly distressing just before going to sleep – a block of flats next to a tram line in Kazan had collapsed that day. Apparently, no one was injured and most of the residents had been at work. It was a really old block of flats and some of the residents being interviewed on the news were saying that they had had concerns about their building for several years and although they had complained to the town council, nothing had been done. The reporter said that the situation had become so bad that it was the heavily rumbling tram that may have caused the block to crumble. In fact, the longer I was in Kazan, the more I realised how common this was. I discovered that many old buildings had collapsed or been pulled down and new blocks were being built in their place. According to some sources, many ethnic Tatars had lived in these old, dilapidated blocks and that the buildings had been left to crumble or had been left until they were in such a state that the residents had had to move out. These buildings were located in historical Tatar districts of the city and there had been plans to re-build some of these districts entirely and transform them into tourist areas complete with hotels, banks, and other commodities.

I managed to get a good night's sleep and at 10am the next morning met Nina in front of Kazan State University. She was an elderly lady with a staunch Soviet mindset, as I discovered when she asked me what the purpose of my research was. I didn't go into too much detail but told her I was interested in the interconnection between identity and language to which she replied that I probably wouldn't find out much because everybody had the same identity in Russia! This was the beginning of me discovering the prevalence of this type of attitude in Kazan and across the post-Soviet space generally. It seemed very chauvinistic – I discovered it was more prevalent among the older population.

I asked Nina if she would speak to Liudmila and Sergei to ask them to register me. Fortunately, she knew why and how I had to register as well as the consequences if I didn't. She took my phone and got Sergei on the other end of the line; he was quite rude to her by all accounts. Nina asked him to put his wife on. Nina explained to her that she needed to meet me at the post office the very next day at 11am to register me. She even explained the consequences to her in no uncertain terms. After she hung up, Nina then started to have a go at me for not allowing her to organise my stay in a university hall of residence. I managed to pacify her, thank her profusely and then she took me along to meet the members of her department who would help me. Later that day I also met Gulnaz who said she could help me to distribute my research questionnaires. She also knew some very influential people in both the Russian and Tatar Academy of Sciences who she could arrange interviews with. I was so grateful. I had met some very hospitable and helpful people on my second day. The only remaining obstacle was the visa registration.

The next morning, I set off to meet Liudmila at 11am at the post office. She was on time and said I had no right to get my university colleague to arrange a meeting or to e-mail her daughter to complain. I just said, "Shall we register?" At the post office counter, I had to do all the talking. The girl at the counter wasn't used to foreigners asking to be registered obviously because of the strange way she looked at me and then at Liudmila who just stood there with a face like a smacked arse. The girl fetched a form for me to fill in and explained that there should be no mistakes and it should be completed in printed Russian letters. I had experience of writing like this in a school where I had once taught Russian and where the languages secretary typed up language learning material worksheets for the students in Russian, although she didn't know any Russian herself.

I was given a pen and the form and Liudmila handed me her passport. She wasn't going to lift a bloody finger to help me. Perhaps she was illiterate. It took me an hour and a half to complete form. Firstly, because I couldn't quite grasp what the form required in some places – it wasn't straight forward. Perhaps it was a method of immigration control to keep foreigners away. Secondly, Liudmila was sat next to me looking disgustingly at my printed Russian writing. She was also tutting and puffing all the time and making me feel nervous, so I started to rush. As a consequence, I kept making mistakes. I had to go back to the girl behind the counter and ask her for more forms. On my third attempt to fill in the form, the girl must have taken pity on me. She called Liudmila over to ask her to help me in an admonishing tone. Liudmila finally snatched the pen out of my hand and completed a few boxes and signed her name. During the time I had been completing the forms, I had felt like just giving up, returning to Sheffield, and packing in my PhD. After all, I had resigned from my teaching job, and I didn't get any help from the university on the visa front. Still, I had held my nerve, I had not broken down in tears and I had made arrangements with academics to carry out my data collection during my stay. The form was completed, the girl stamped it and gave me a slip of paper telling me that it was my registration document and that I should keep with my passport and mustn't lose it at all costs. I handed back Liudmila's passport to her and she swung around on her stilettos and stormed off and out of the post office! I didn't see her again until the last week of my stay, thank goodness.

As a legal alien I could now continue with my purpose of collecting research data. In fact, I had a really successful time in Kazan interviewing people, meeting students and managed to get all my surveys completed for data collection analysis when I returned to Sheffield in November. I kept in touch with all my contacts and I'm still in touch with them to this very day. I made subsequent research trips to Kazan and conferences in Moscow during my PhD.

The following weekend Nastya showed me around the Kazan Kremlin complex and the Tatar Settlement district, which was an ethnic Tatar area where many mosques were situated as well as old wooden houses. There were shells of buildings that used to belong to Tatar merchants, and manufacturers. I noticed that many of the wooden buildings had burned down. Nastya didn't know why the buildings were so dilapidated. In fact, there were many buildings around Kazan city centre that had been abandoned and left to ruin. Just the shells of once palatial buildings remained, covered in graffiti with weeds growing out of where rooms and apartments had once been occupied, but which were now full of rubbish from fly-tipping.

*Figure 5: Accommodation on Rakhmatullin Street*

The reason for this dilapidation, which I discovered later, was that the first president of post-Soviet Tatarstan, called Mintimir Shaimev, had ordered a 'Program for Slum Clearance and Modernization of Slum Areas (1995-2004)'. Many old historical buildings had been deemed 'unsafe' or 'unfit to live in'. Many people had to leave their homes so that the buildings they lived in could be knocked down and replaced by newer buildings. The people who had lived in such buildings were offered new apartments in other parts of the city. Many citizens of Kazan argued that their history was being destroyed. However, at that time I was told that the government had run out of money for the slum clearance project and there were many half broken-down buildings in the centre of Kazan that had just been left, which explained why the buildings were in such a state of dilapidation. The first president of Tatarstan commissioned many new buildings to be built, which reflected the multicultural (Tatar) aspects of the city, such as the Kul Sharif Mosque built inside the Kremlin walls, which was given as a gift to the Muslim Tatar people by President Shaimev and was as a symbol of Tatarstan's sovereignty at that time.

*Figure 6: Kul Sharif Mosque and Pyramid Hotel*

Other mosques around the city were renovated or rebuilt. National Tatar monuments and museums were also erected.

During a second trip to Kazan in April-June 2013 many of the old, derelict buildings I had witnessed during my visit in 2010 had been rebuilt. In the Tatar settlement area, some of the historical Tatar buildings had been transformed into hotels and banks for the student games. I felt that this was a sign of globalisation finally reaching Kazan. The city seemed to have been transformed from a derelict city of the post-Soviet space into a global city of the future.

However, when I returned in 2017 purely to visit Gulnaz and Nastya, the Tatar Settlement district had been further transformed into what appeared to be a Tatar Disneyland. Many houses had been rebuilt and repainted in garish bright colours. Shiney golden plaques had been placed on the walls of the building to commemorate the people who had once lived there such as poets, writers, and influential merchants.

As result of the successful bid for the 2018 football World Cup in Russia, more money had been donated to Kazan from the Russian central government to reconstruct and finish its buildings and roads in order to make it into a more international and global city. Some of the main streets in the Tatar Settlement district had been pedestrianised. There were also several hotels and banks which tourists would stay in. A Tatar museum had been housed in one of the buildings and many of the previously burned buildings had been turned into Tatar heritage museums, which portrayed the Tatar way of life as being more *agricultural* and *rural* than as part of a functioning contemporary society. Another building I saw near the Kazan Kremlin had been converted into a beer house. I went to have a look and saw familiar brands of bottled beers from the UK and Europe. There was an air of superficiality about it. I wondered what would become of the hotels and the western style bars after the World cup. There were clearly no locals in these places.

I haven't been back since 2017 and it is impossible at the moment with the war in Ukraine.

## Chapter 10: Stock Cubes

*"Do you want to buy a stock cube?"* the man asked.

*"Sorry, can you repeat that please?"* I replied disbelievingly.

Again, he asked if I wanted to buy a stock cube. I replied, *"No, thank you."* Out of one of the pockets of his brown leather-look bomber jacket he pulled out a pack of *Knorr* chicken stock cubes and asked, *"Don't you need one? Come on, just nineteen rubles."* Again, I replied that I didn't need a stock cube. He then looked at me and said, *"Are you from Poland?"* I said no, I was from England.

This conversation happened to me one morning in May 2013 on the outskirts of Kazan while waiting for my colleague, Gulnaz, who was notoriously late every time we arranged to meet up. On one occasion, I had to wait two hours for her to turn up. Why didn't I just walk off, you ask. Well, she was the gatekeeper to all my interviews for my research data, which she had organised with many of her colleagues working in academic research institutes in Kazan. I needed to wait for her in order to get to these institutes so that I could distribute my research questionnaires to students in lectures with the help of her colleagues.

On this particular morning, I left my friend Nastya's apartment and took the bus with instructions to get off at such and such bus stop, cross the road and wait by the kiosk on the corner of the street. So, I followed these orders. Gulnaz had arranged to drive to the corner of the street and pick me up in order to take me to the Institute of Law in Kazan. She was supposed to pick me up at 10am and so I waited, waited, and waited. Fortunately, it was sunny, and the temperature had already reached the mid-twenties by that time in the morning. Gulnaz phoned me about 10:20 and told me that she was *just* setting off from her home on the other side of the city and that she wouldn't take long to get to me, depending on the traffic. So, I waited patiently. And I waited and waited. I felt rather uncomfortable stood on the street corner and it must have looked obvious that I was either deranged, a prostitute or a foreigner. As I waited, I noticed a man walking up the street towards me. He was wearing a brown leather-look bomber jacket, trousers (thankfully) and a black woolly hat, which seemed strange given that the temperature was in the mid-twenties (above zero). I could see him looking at me as he was walking up the street. I decided to look around me and keep checking my watch to make it look as if I was waiting for somebody.

He approached me and tried to sell me a stock cube. After this initial conversation opener, he started to ask why I was stood on the street corner, so I proceeded to explain that I was waiting for a colleague to come and pick me up. He asked me what I was doing in Kazan, and I told him that I was doing research into language use. He kept nodding his head as if he was interested in my research. I then plucked up courage to ask him why he was trying to sell stock cubes. He said he needed the money for a bus ticket to get to the rehabilitation centre where he had an appointment. The price of the bus fare was nineteen rubles. He then pulled off his woolly black hat revealing a bald head and a huge scar from back to front, which must have been about one centimetre wide and smaller scars where the stitches had been. He said he was an Afghan war veteran and was receiving help for drug and alcohol addiction at the rehabilitation centre, which was where he was going that morning to attend an appointment, but he didn't have any money for the bus.

The Soviet Afghan war happened between 1978 and 1989 on the territory of Afghanistan. It was the longest military operation up to that point in history. The aim of the 'military operation' was to protect the Afghan people from invasive aggressors – in other words, from the west (sounds familiar, doesn't it?). According to the official figures of the Soviet government, over 620,000 Soviet soldiers and more than 21,000 civilians were deployed in Afghanistan. In 1989, the reported death toll of Soviet soldiers was 13,933 and 469,685 were wounded. 10,751 were classed as invalids on their return to a politically, socially, and economically disintegrating country[27]. Many soldiers who returned had been radicalised by their experiences and turned against the Soviet system.

The Afghan veterans were treated with disdain upon their return and blamed for the war in Afghanistan by a large section of Soviet society who had been uninformed by the Soviet media. The media would occasionally report on how the Soviet troops were protecting the Afghans from the US, British and Pakistani empires and would portray the Soviet troops as peacekeepers. As a result of this peaceful representation, soldiers and their families could not claim any special privileges upon their return home. This included conscripts, non-commissioned officers as well as professional officers. This 'politics of concealment' even extended to those killed during the war whose tombstones were not allowed to reveal the real cause of death. Their coffins were spread out across local cemeteries to hide their public visibility. Consequently, the soldiers' families could not claim any benefits. Mikhail Gorbachev would later claim that the Soviet Afghan war had been a mistake.

The history of social benefits of war veterans in Russia can be traced back to the time of the 1917 Revolution. Social and political policy were intertwined, and social benefits were considered instrumental in the social hierarchical political system at that time. Privileges were awarded to Party members and workers. Social benefits extended to members of the armed forces and conscription was re-introduced in 1918 because it was an effective means of mobilisation. It was considered an honour to be called up to serve in the military service. However, many citizens were excluded from this system due to their social background, profession, qualifications, and past activities. This changed in 1936 under Stalin's Constitution, which stated that all citizens had equal rights. As a result of a military law passed in 1939, all Soviet male citizens had to serve in the military. This law remained unchanged until 1994.

After the Second World War, Soviet veterans acquired a privileged status. They were entitled to the free cost of transport home from the battlefields as well as food for the journey, a set of clothes, shoes, and a cash lump sum calculated on army pay and length of service. They were also entitled to privileges in education, employment, and pensions.

Despite these privileges immediately following the Second World War, in 1947 all veterans' benefits were abolished because Stalin wanted to claim all the victory for himself. This was part of Stalin's long-running campaign to re-write the history of World War II. Hence, many veterans went to work in cities across the Soviet Union as part of the Soviet industrialisation programme. Some worked in administrative positions in local government management systems.

In the 1960s under Krushchev's rule, World War II veterans were able to receive welfare benefits once again and were eventually given privileges in housing, health, free transport, tax allowances, and nursing allowances for the severely disabled. They were also entitled to an annual trip to a health resort.

In contrast, the Afghan veterans were not given the same benefits as the veterans of the Great Patriotic War (as World War II had been re-named) and were labelled differently[28]. Veterans of the Great Patriotic War were the only veterans who had exclusive rights to welfare benefits and were an exclusively elite group. In 1985 the Soviet media started to construct a heroic discourse of the Afghan war. This led to Afghan war veterans being allowed to claim special welfare benefits. Despite this step forward, claiming benefits was a lengthy process due to unclear policy documentation and implementation. Many Afghan veterans did not receive the benefits they had been promised. This was also due to the lack of government resources and health programmes to deal with the specialist requirements of this population. Most of the benefits were on paper only. These Afghan war veterans suffered from post-traumatic stress disorder (PTSD), alcohol and drug abuse, crime, family problems, and suicides. At that time there were not enough trained mental health specialists for PTSD and the hospitals where PTSD patients were treated were viewed negatively by the war veterans as a punishment rather than as therapy. Many veterans therefore did not seek help and others did not want 'alcoholic' stamped on their identity cards[29].

After the collapse of the Soviet Union, three large veterans' organisations were set up and granted privileges. These were the Union of Afghan Veterans, the Russian Union of Afghan War Veterans, and the Russian Foundation for Disabled Afghan War Veterans. The Russian welfare system was in crisis by the end of the 1990s and many veterans did not receive their benefits. The benefits had gone to the private interests of the veterans' leaders. The collapse of this system due to corruption left insufficient provisions for veterans and only added to their devalued status. Social media groups for Afghan war veterans were set up on *VKontakte* for veterans to express their feelings about their treatment and lack of benefits. Clubs were also set up by the Afghan veterans to help and support each other. These clubs served as bases for activism for human rights to get their plight recognised by the outside world. They also provided self-help such as readjustment counselling, physiotherapy, and massage therapy.

I decided that I didn't want a stock cube, but I gave him 100 rubles. He was extremely grateful, and I could only hope that he really was going to the rehabilitation centre. After this he went down the street hopefully to a bus stop and my colleague Gulnaz pulled up at the side of the road. I got into the car, and she apologised for being late. I told her about my conversation with the war veteran and she told me that I shouldn't speak to strangers!

**Part 5**

**Georgia**

Georgia is a multi-ethnic country and is situated in the South Caucasus. It shares its borders with the Russian Federation in the north and northeast, Armenia and Turkey in the south, Azerbaijan in the southeast and is situated on the eastern side of the Black Sea. Tbilisi is the capital city. The main religions practised in Georgia are Georgian Christian Orthodox, Muslim, and Armenian Apostolic. Its geopolitical positioning has been the root of several conflicts and wars with the Russian Federation since the collapse of the Soviet Union. Following this collapse in 1991, the Georgian government aimed to reunify its population through the use of Georgian as the state language as one of its nation-building processes. Georgian was declared as the state language and Russian lost its status as the language of interethnic communication after 1991.

The Georgian language became compulsory in all schools for all nationalities, but this was a problem in certain districts of Georgia where many ethnic minorities lived compactly together; for example, the Armenian population in Samtskhe-Javakheti and the Azeri population in Kvemo Kartli. Armenian and Russian have remained the dominant languages in the Samtskhe-Javakheti district and Azeri and Russian in

Kvemo Kartli despite the fact that Georgian is the state language. Since the collapse of the USSR various leaders of the Georgian government have attempted to improve multilingual education for ethnic minorities as a means to help them 'integrate' into Georgian society. My task, therefore, was to examine how effective multilingual educational reforms had been in Georgia in helping ethnic minorities integrate into Georgian society during the post-Soviet period and uncover the hidden language ideologies at play.

The focus of the multilingual educational reforms was on the Armenian and Azeri ethnic groups because they were the largest ethnic minority groups in Georgia. According to the preliminary results of the 2014 population census, the Azeris comprise 6.3% of the total population and the Armenians comprise 4.5%. Other large ethnic groups in Georgia include Russians (0.7%), and Ossetians (0.4%). Historically, both Armenian and Azeri settlements in Georgia were the result of external aggressive forces and conflicts, such as the Ottoman Turks and Iranians. These nationalities fled persecution and settled in Georgia near the borders of their historic homelands where they still reside to this day, as well as in Tbilisi.

## Chapter 11: The Banya

During my first trip to Georgia in 2015, I was based in Tbilisi and had booked a small hotel close to the city centre just next to the Azeri ethnic district called Abanotubani. The hotel room had a balcony with views of the Mtkvari river and the orthodox church on the opposite side of the street. Occasionally, a priest would emerge from the church, get into his expensive four-by-four SUV and drive off to carry out his daily rituals. Obviously, the car came with the job.

The hotel served delicious breakfasts of Georgian fare including *khachapuri*, a type of cheesy flatbread with a poached egg on top, as well as fresh fruit and other pastries. The hotel was family run and the owners were very kind and helpful. However, as was the case at that time, whole districts of cities and towns were prone to power blackouts and intermittent water supplies.

One morning I woke up to discover there was no running water in the hotel. My initial reaction was panic – I was going to be carrying out interviews later that day in Tbilisi at a non-governmental organisation (NGO) and didn't think it was a good idea to turn up looking like somebody who had tried to fry an egg on their head as this would give a bad impression. So, I threw on some clothes and went to reception to ask when the water was likely to come back on. The receptionist, who was the hotel owner's son and on reception duty that morning, seemed non-plussed when I asked him and said he didn't know, but there was a good *banya* (bath house) down the road, which was not expensive. He said many people went there when there was no running water. I decided that I had no choice but to go there because I needed to be presentable later that day. I gathered my swimming costume, small towel, other toiletries, and set off.

The banya were situated in the mainly Azeri ethnic district called Abanotubani adjacent to the river and were an amazing site to behold. Red-brick dome-shaped bath house roofs protruded out of the ground with air vents on the top of each dome to let out the hot steam.

*Figure 7: Banya district*

The banya had been built on the hot sulphurous springs that ran underground in Tbilisi. According to local legend, King Vakhtang Gorgasali discovered the hot springs while out hunting with his falcon and ordered the capital city to be built around this spot, which he called *tbili* (meaning warm) and from which the name Tbilisi originated. A monument in honour of Gorgasali can be found on the opposite riverbank and was visible from my balcony at the hotel. The banya date back to the fifth century and there were many more than what there are today. Travellers used to stop off at the banya to take the waters, including Pushkin who wrote an epithet about the banya and how much he enjoyed them, which is now written on a plaque on the outside of the Orbeliana banya. As well as travellers and the locals coming to wash at the banya, I was informed that mothers would go to check out their future daughter-in-laws for defects. Fortunately, this no longer happens and the banya are visited more by expats and tourists than they are by the local population. Many of the workers were of Azeri ethnic origin and the banya were gender segregated.

I had been given a recommendation for the best banya to visit, but when I arrived in the area, I ended up getting lost among the dome-shaped roofs and entered one with an elaborately tiled entrance hoping it would be fine. Inside I found myself in a white-tiled hallway with a counter behind which were many shelves stacked with towels. There was a strong smell of ironing and sulphur, and it was very humid. I approached the counter and saw a woman who was folding up towels that had been freshly washed. She asked what I wanted, and I told her I would like a private bathroom for an hour. I had been advised it was best to ask for a private bathroom. Although we both conversed in Russian, she could see that I was a foreigner and the currency signs started to kerching in her eyes. It was going to cost me eighty Georgian lari for the private room, plus an additional fee for a *kisi* scrub and some tea. It did not seem like I had a choice in the matter, although I told her I had my own towel. She handed me a receipt, came out from behind the counter and told me to follow her downstairs. She led me down a dimly lit corridor and opened a heavy wooden door, which led into a 'sitting' area. It was a large room with several black leather sofas and a coffee table. The sofas looked a bit worse for wear and were a little grimy. The walls were covered in white tiles but looked like they were yellowing from age, or the sulphur. The woman showed me around the bathing area, which was in the adjoining room. There were various bathtubs of hot and cold sulphur waters, the shower and the *kisi* scrub room in the back corner with a marble slab inside. It looked like a medieval sacrificial table. She told me to lock the door behind her, but that the *kisi* masseuse would be along after about ten minutes, so I would need to let her in.

I locked the door and proceeded to get undressed, shower and then bathe. I was really looking forward to a relaxing bath and had just immersed myself in the hot spring tub when there was a loud, heavy knocking at the door. It sounded like the mafia had arrived on the other side of the door and I was petrified. I quickly jumped out of the bathtub and put on my swimming costume. I unlocked the door to find an old lady with a scarf wrapped around her head and a blue plastic bucket in her hand. She smiled at me revealing her silver and gold teeth and introduced herself as my masseuse. I invited her in, and she made her way to the back room where the marble slab was situated. I locked the door behind her, relieved that it was not the mafia after all, and followed her into the sacrificial chamber. She asked me to remove my swimming costume and lie on the marble slab. She put the bucket under a tap and began to fill it. I noticed a kind of plastic scouring pad on a ledge along with a squeezy plastic bottle filled with some liquid. She asked me where I was from and what I was doing in Georgia - all the usual questions. She then explained that she would wash me first before the exfoliation. I really did not have a clue what to expect and I was at her mercy. Before she began, she excused herself for a minute, went to a hole in the floor in the corner of the chamber, lifted her skirt, revealing that she was wearing no knickers, squatted, and pissed into the hole. She then let her skirt down, clapped her hands in glee and walked towards the bucket. She must have been dying for a wee. She picked up the bucket and threw its contents at me, which was quite warm, thankfully. She then proceeded to wash me with a sponge, first on my front, then on my back. After about five minutes, she asked me to sit up, took the squeezy bottle and scouring pad from the ledge and started to squirt pink liquid all over me. She then took the scouring pad and began scrubbing my arms then legs. It was quite painful, and I was sure she had reached my second epidermis. She stopped, filled up the bucket with water again and then threw it at me. It was freezing! I had not expected that. She cackled at my shocked expression and asked if I would like to do it again. I said no, it was enough. Just at that moment, somebody started banging on the door again. This time, the masseuse went to answer it and let in the tea lady. The masseuse left and the tea lady followed. I had no idea how long I had been in there or had left. I thought that I could finally relax in the warm bathtub again with a cup of tea. I arranged the tea tray on the edge of the bath and once again immersed myself in the warm sulphuric water. As soon as I had immersed myself, somebody else started banging on the door. I couldn't believe it! Once again, I got out and asked who it was.

The person on the other side of the door shouted that I had ten minutes left and I had to get out. I hurriedly tried to dry myself on the small hand towel I had brought with me and noticed quite a lot of blood on the towel. I wondered what it was but then discovered that my index finger had been deeply scratched by the masseuse's scouring pad. I wrapped the towel around my finger to stem the flow of blood and threw on my clothes. I gathered my possessions and opened the door to see an assistant waiting to take me back to the reception upstairs. As I followed her out, she asked if I would like my hair doing pointing at a row of women sat on wooden benches in front of a row of mirrors. They were all looking at me, smiling as if they could squeeze a bit more currency out of me. I politely declined the offer and went back to the counter upstairs to settle my bill. The woman behind the counter totted up the so-called treatments I had had, which came to five hundred *lari* in total – an absolute abomination! I decided to just pay and get the hell out of there. I ran back to the hotel and finished getting ready for my interviews that afternoon.

My finger was still bleeding later that day I decided that I would not go back to the banya after that experience. Fortunately, the water came back on later that evening. I have still got the scar on my index finger to this very day, and I still have visions of the masseuse having a piss in the corner of the sacrificial chamber.

## Chapter 12: Health and Safety

During my first trip to Georgia as a consultant, I was tasked with visiting many schools and interviewing as many teachers as possible in both the Armenian and Azeri regions of the country. This particular account is about one of those trips in the Azeri region.

I was driven there by the organisation's driver and was also accompanied by the project assistant who acted as negotiator and Georgian interpreter when necessary. We set off about 8:30 in the morning on a three-hour drive to the district in which the school was situated. The countryside was stunningly beautiful with lush green hills bordering the surprisingly complete roads. The landscape in this part of Georgia was different to the one I had witnessed in the Armenian region. It was not so rugged and there were more hills than mountains at the start of our journey. There was not much traffic – it was early in the day for Georgians who generally do not start work until about 10am. I had not had any breakfast for this reason - the hotel breakfast buffet did not open until 9:30. Furthermore, I had had very little to drink – I was told that public toilets did not exist and that school toilets were a no-go zone.

I was growing accustomed to sights that would have seemed amusing or shocking to anyone who had not stepped foot inside the country before. Cattle were wandering in the middle of the road with their herders as if there was absolutely no rush to get anywhere at all – and why should there have been?

*Figure 8: Cattle wandering the streets*

In one town we passed through, there were many cattle all over the streets and they were conglomerating around a public drinking fountain. This was not just for the cattle, I should add. People were also stood next to the fountain with buckets waiting for their turn to fill up. There were also large groups of men in black leather-look bomber jackets sitting around on stools drinking tea, smoking, spitting on the pavement, and playing backgammon and chess.

I couldn't see any women on the streets. Perhaps they were at home with their daughters, either preparing them for marriage or celebrating recent marriage ceremonies. I noticed that many of the houses along the streets were hidden behind high brick walls with large, reinforced metal security gates. On many of the gates red flowers and bows were hung. When I asked the project assistant why this was, she told me that many Azeri families marry their daughters off at a very young age, rather too young in fact. As it turned out, it was illegal for anybody to marry under the age of sixteen in Georgia. I was also told that it was not unusual for young girls to be kidnapped and taken away to be married. This was therefore another reason why the houses we passed had very high walls and reinforced security gates.

I discovered that there existed many gender issues in Azeri ethnic minority villages regarding education, participation in civic life in addition to early marriage. Two reasons for this are the cultural setting and Muslim traditions. Girls were generally only expected to receive basic education at primary level. The number of girls who attended primary school was higher than that of boys, but the gender balance shifted considerably by the time the children graduated from the school system. This was because of the role the family played in a girl's destiny – any education higher than the basic level was considered pointless because the role of the girls was in the home. Many girls worked in agriculture or within the home until they were married off. Therefore, higher level education above primary level was regarded as no use.

Apparently, several awareness workshops had taken place in this region of Georgia in order to try to make the population aware that it was illegal for girls under sixteen to marry. As a result of these workshops, not as many underage girls were getting married and some were even staying on at school beyond the age of fourteen to get an education. In recent years there has been an increase in the number of girls who have continued beyond basic education and graduated from Georgian universities. Workshops were also run to raise the awareness of learning the Georgian language as a means of socio-economic advancement within Georgia for both adults and children of both genders.

As well as language barriers, there had been many financial barriers to continuing educational possibilities for both genders. However, in recent years, the Azeri oil company called SOCAR has been providing funding for those Azeri children who pass their school exams.

The only way to access higher education courses is through Georgian-medium education. In order for the Ministry of Education and Science (MoES) to include ethnic minorities in higher education, a Georgian language access course for ethnic minority students was created called the 1 + 4 programme. The 1 + 4 programme refers to an initiative that enables ethnic minority students in Georgia to enrol on university courses. Currently the quota for enrolment of ethnic minorities is 12% of the total places available at universities: 5% each from Armenian and Azeri ethnic minority populations and 1% each from the Ossetian and Abkhazian ethnic minority populations. These students must pass the general skills tests in their own native language before acceptance onto the programme. Once these tests are passed, these students follow a one-year intensive Georgian language programme that prepares them to pass the university entrance exams and enrol on bachelor's programmes for a further four years. The 1 + 4 programme was regarded by everybody who participated in my research to have been successful in raising the number of ethnic minority students applying for university places within Georgia. Azeri ethnic communities have reaped the rewards of higher education within their communities. This is because many Azeri graduates have returned to their communities after graduating to educate their local communities and to set up their own businesses and projects for young people to take part in and to make their voices heard. For example, in Marneuli, a large city in the Kvemo Kartli region of Georgia where approximately half of the population is of Azeri origin, a peer-led youth project was set up called 'From Youth for Youth'. Young people wanted to integrate more with other ethnic groups and came together through shared musical interests and started to learn Georgian as a means to communicate with each other. Another project that brought people together was the broadcasting of an ethnic minority radio station that was run by young people from mixed ethnic groups for the ethnic minorities. The British Broadcasting Company (BBC) World Service Trust set up this project. Unfortunately, the National Commission for Broadcasting and Communications in Georgia withheld the license because they did not have the funding to continue this project and there was not enough continued interest in the project from other organisations. Another issue for the Azeri population was that they had very little opportunity to participate in civic life in Georgia. This was due to the language barrier and therefore the lack of opportunity to participate in Georgian civil society.

We passed through the town and continued our drive towards the school along the mountain passes and roads. So many of the roads had collapsed in places due to heavy rainfall and landslides or through neglect. It was scary when we met with oncoming traffic on the same side of the road around hairpin bends at speed. However, drivers here were obviously used to such events and always got around the potholes and oncoming trucks just in the nick of time. Nobody flinched. After some time, I also grew accustomed to this way of driving and found myself thrilled after near collisions.

It was a shame to see so much trash dumped at the foot of some of these magnificent mountains. Plastic waste, building materials and I dread to think what else. I think workshops on cleaning up the environment were also necessary, but that was not my task.

As we approached the village where the school was situated, more snow started to appear, and the temperature dropped. The driver was still driving at breakneck speed. As we drove through the village, I noticed the villagers would stop what they were doing and turn to look at the car. They recognised it and genuinely looked pleased to see it. They associated it with much needed help from the outside world. We approached a school enclosed by high wrought iron gates. The school was framed against a backdrop of high mountains covered in snow and white fluffy clouds surrounding the peaks. We stopped outside of the gates as a man approached to open them. We slowly drove in. He gave us a welcoming smile as we stepped out of the car onto the snowy playground. He led us across the playground towards the main school building, which was painted in faded yellow and white. On my right-hand side at a distance, I saw a group of people stood around something and singing. I wondered what was happening and went closer. As I approached, I could not believe my eyes. A group of very young boys, about eight to ten years of age, had formed a circle around a bonfire, which seemed to be made up of old broken school furniture, branches and whatever else had been found lying around. All of the boys were stood around the fire singing and clapping in unison but taking it in turns to jump over the fire! There was a teacher with them who was encouraging them to jump and blowing a whistle for the next boy to take his turn. None of the boys was wearing a winter coat. I presumed that this was because the fire was keeping them warm. They all looked happy and were having fun at least. The thought that came to my mind was, would this be allowed as a playtime activity in schools across the UK? This type of activity would certainly build up stamina. Had a risk assessment taken place? Were their clothes fireproof? Had a letter of permission been sent to the boys' parents? Anyway, it was time to go in and meet the headteacher and I was freezing. I was actually thinking that it would have been better to join in with the bonfire activity than do my interview. So, we entered the school and the usual whiff of cabbage, asbestos and piss hit my nostrils. We were led up the stairs to the headteacher's office. I noticed that the corridor and the stairs were covered in exotic-looking blue patterned tiles all the way to the headteacher's office door. As I looked to my right down other school corridors, I noticed that the builders had not finished the floor tiling. The floors there were just made of old brown concrete covered in dirt. It was also freezing inside the school. We entered the headteacher's office, which was furnished with thick rugs and comfortable sofas as well as the headteacher's desk. I must mention the head teacher's desk! As is usual in all the schools and universities I have ever entered in eastern Europe and beyond, the desk was set out with the head teacher at the helm and another long thin table joining this main desk to form a 'T' shape. Guests and teachers would be seated along this table as the minions. The head teacher's desk was often covered with framed family photos and certificates as well as trophies and other educational awards. Behing the head teacher's chair (or throne) on the wall would be hung a large photo of the leader or president of the country. This school was no exception. There was also a glass cabinet, which contained sample textbooks and posters from non-governmental organisations who, by the kindness of their hearts had donated free materials to the school to help the students (and teachers) learn Georgian.

Another thing that struck me in this room was the heat. It hit me like a brick wall. The headteacher had his own wood burning stove! No need for him to jump over a bonfire then!

The rest of the day was spent listening to the concerns of the Azeri teachers in the school. They were all wrapped up in hats, scarves, and gloves. No wonder break time activities were focused on warming up! On the way out I checked to see if the boys were still jumping over the bonfire – I would definitely have joined in this time – unfortunately, they had all gone home, and the fire had been put out. I really thought at the time that the school would benefit more from a heating system rather than NGO textbooks that were never even opened.

## Chapter 12: The Cat Lady of Sioni Street, Tbilisi

If you happened to be in Tbilisi anytime during 2015, you probably came across the cat lady of Sioni Street. You couldn't really miss her. She appeared to be quite elderly, or maybe it was the lifestyle of a homeless woman that made her appear elderly. She was wrapped up in multiple layers of long coats, and woolly jumpers and wearing a pair of battered old trainers on her feet, which had holes under the soles. Her sleeping arrangements were in the doorway of a disused boarded-up building on Sioni street a few doors down from the carpet maker shop. When I saw her for the very first time, she was asleep in the doorway, laid out on her back, her head resting on a stone slab for a pillow. On top of her were three stray cats curled up and sleeping, keeping her warm or vice versa. There was another cat curled up by her feet and another that looked like it was standing guard in one of the broken windows of the building overlooking the old lady and her companions. There were several pouches of *Whiskers* and *Kit-e-Kat* cat food slotted in between the cracks of the building and the gaps between the window frames and the outer wall. I wondered whether the pouches were provided by the old lady or passers-by.

*Figure 9: The Cat Lady of Sioni Street*

At least the cats were being fed. I wondered what the old lady ate – perhaps the cat food as well. It was quite a distressing sight to behold, and I decided to keep walking along this street quite often during my stay here to see if the old lady spent much time in this doorway.

I continued walking along Sioni Street until I came to a turning into a small interesting looking pedestrian alleyway full of restaurants, bars, cafes, and nightclubs. It seemed to be a surprisingly upmarket area of Tbilisi, obviously with tourists and wealthy clientele in mind. However, as I continued walking down the alleyway, I couldn't help but notice the sheer abundance of stray cats and kittens. Everywhere. Cats of all shapes and sizes, scuttling around for scraps of food, sleeping on the outdoor furniture of the cafes and restaurants. The cats were all strays and were in a variety of conditions. I remember one very small black and white cat in particular, skulking in a doorway, which had seen better days, as one of its ears looked like it had been brutally savaged - in fact on closer inspection, its ear was missing.

*Figure 10: One of Tbilisi's Stray Cats*

It was awful, I couldn't help but feel distressed at this sight and the delight of discovering such an upmarket area of Tbilisi soon left me. As a cat lover, with two of my own back home, I wanted to adopt them all and wondered why there were so many in such deplorable conditions.

I had reached the end of the alleyway and ended up at Meidan Palace, a square through which the road over the Metekhi bridge ran to get to down-town Tbilisi from the other side of the river. I had to cross this square to get back to my hotel, taking care not to be savaged by packs of stray dogs, fleeced of money by groups of beggars and their bedraggled children shouting *Madonnochka* (Madonna) at me as I hurriedly walk past, or being knocked over by the relentless traffic passing through the square.

In all cities and towns of the post-Soviet space I have visited over the years, I have noticed many stray animals, dogs in particular. They are usually a sandy colour, manky, and can be found on street corners, grass verges, outside kiosks, everywhere. They are usually seen together in packs and very rarely alone. They are part of the landscape and often affectionately called 'Sharik' with reference to Mikhael Bulgakov's satirical novel *The Heart of a Dog* in which a doctor takes a stray dog into his home, feeds it, cares for it, before operating on it and changing it into a human being. This isn't without consequences, of course, as the dog-man lives a miserable life among humans, wishing to be changed back into a dog.

Stray dogs in the post-Soviet space are generally well tolerated within the public landscape. Occasionally, somebody may emerge from the entrance of a block of flats and throw the dogs some left-over meat, which the dogs totally appreciate. However, if you go to Georgia, stray animals take on a whole new meaning.

It can be dangerous if you come across a large pack of dogs, particularly at night in Tbilisi. Food couriers are often followed by stray dogs sniffing out a potential meal, and if couriers are not careful, the dogs can snatch packets of food from them. The dogs can get aggressive and bite. There is a problem with rabies in Georgia and it is therefore better not to go where there are packs of dogs, let alone be followed by them.

I discovered later that many dogs are abandoned by their owners in Georgia. This is due to not being able to afford to keep a dog or afford a trip to the vets. Residents cannot afford to get their pets spayed or neutered, so when a new litter is born, many of the animals are abandoned. In Tbilisi, unwanted dogs are taken to the outskirts of the city or to the countryside and just left there. As there was no requirement to register dogs in Georgia at that time, nobody cared what happened to them and they just multiplied.

Animal cruelty was also a problem in Georgia. Dog fighting was a popular sport, and the fights were often recorded and posted on social media platforms. Furthermore, animals were captured and killed tortuously with the use of guns, physical abuse, strangling, starvation and hanging – as sporting activities. The carcasses disappeared and nobody knew where to. There was no law enforcement on such cruel activities. There was a general lack of awareness about animal rights and animal protection, which seems shocking in the twenty-first century.

The Georgian Society for the Protection and Safety of Animals (GSPSA) was set up in 2006. It managed to set up animal shelters in Georgia, but there was a lack of state funding due to poverty issues in the country. The GSPSA claimed that the deplorable animal situation in the country was due to government mistakes such as a lack of disease control, misuse of state funds, and the mass systematic culling of stray animals using unacceptable and cruel methods.

However, under the influence and pressure of international and local non-governmental organisations, the charity *Animal Shelter* was founded in 2012. The aim of the charity was to prevent animal cruelty and to try to manage the stray animal population more humanely. A few actions and laws were implemented, although this did not have much effect on attitudes towards animals. Education programmes were set up to try to raise awareness about animal rights and protection across society, but animal cruelty continued to be practised.

An educational campaign to inform and communicate with the population was conducted between 2013-2017. Educational materials on animal cruelty and the risk of rabies were distributed in schools and among the population. However, not all target groups were covered during this awareness campaign, and the campaign had little effect on the management of the animal population.

In 2015, a law was passed "On the approval of rules for the maintenance of animals (dogs, cats) and the management of their population in the Tbilisi municipality". Many volunteers came to offer their services from outside of Georgia and help with the situation. Facebook groups were set up for monetary donations to help buy food for the animals and to pay for vaccinations, neutering and spaying.

In 2017, there were 52,008 animal bites recorded to humans, but no deaths, according to *fondation-merieux.org*. This organisation established a mass rabies vaccination programme across Georgia and in 2017, 264,398 domestic dogs and cats were vaccinated against rabies as well as 3,440 stray dogs in Tbilisi. Another national awareness campaign was run in 2022, which involved all regional centres of Georgia with the event being broadcast on TV and radio.

Although the situation is far from under complete control in Georgia, laws were implemented to make it compulsory to register a domestic animal, get it chipped, spayed, or neutered. Many charities, which were set up across Georgia, provided these services for free.

As a result of these rabies vaccination programmes and awareness campaigns, cases of rabies in animals have been reduced by 66%, according to the Global Alliance for Rabies Control. Animal owners are also taking more responsibility for their pets. Instead of buying a new animal, members of the public are adopting street animals and giving them a home. This can only help the situation and the awareness campaigns should continue.

I returned to Tbilisi in October 2016 to present my research findings to the Georgian government and other agencies. One afternoon I had a casual stroll down Sioni Street to see if the cat lady was around. This was obviously some time before the animal awareness and rabies campaign had started. The doorway where the cat lady had slept was devoid of life. I could only see one empty pouch of Whiskers slotted in a crack of the building wall. It looked like the step had been swept and the building was probably on the verge of being turned into a trendy new hotel. I was both sad and happy – sad because of the impending doom of yet another possible new hotel full of ignorant tourists to the city. I was happy in the hope that cat lady and her companions had found a home of their own.

# Part 6

# Ukraine

**Chapter 13: Food for Thought**

In August 2014, after the Luhansk and Donbass regions in the east of Ukraine were occupied by Russian forces, a volunteer group from these regions, called *Food for Life*, was set up to help the disabled, elderly and others in need[30].

This organisation provided hot, vegan meals, medical supplies, and PPE. All donations made to the organisation were passed directly onto volunteers working in the occupied territories of Ukraine.

One of these volunteers was called Oksana, although I had met her long before the trubles began. We met in early 2010 on an online conversation exchange platform via Skype. I was due to go to Russia later that year to carry out some data collection for my doctoral research and I needed to get my Russian back into shape. I hadn't spoken it for a few years and was lacking in confidence. My perimenopause had started at the age of thirty-eight and this didn't do much for my confidence either. Oksana was an English teacher and wanted to keep her English-speaking skills up to date. We arranged a time to chat online, and that was the beginning of a long friendship, which continues to this very day.

Oksana lives in Alchevsk, a town in the Luhansk region of Ukraine. The town had a large metallurgy plant, where approximately 10,000 people worked. Oksana did some translation work for the plant from time to time, but her main job was as an English teacher. She taught groups of private students and individuals in her apartment. Oksana lived with her husband Maxim and daughter Lily, who was twelve years old when Oksana and I first began our friendship. A couple of years after we started chatting online, and we even had a chance to meet up face-to-face in 2011 when Oksana came to the UK to do an intensive English course at the University of Leeds.

However, a couple of years later after her first trip to the UK, Oksana took a group of school children, including her daughter, to Ireland for a summer camp. When she returned to Ukraine with the group later that summer, they took a train from Kyiv to the Luhansk region where they were from but were stopped at the Luhansk territorial border by guards, who needed to do a thorough check of everybody in Oksana's group before allowing them to cross the border and return home. They had to stay on the train for several nights. This was the beginning of a new and disturbing existence for Oksana and many others in the Luhansk and Donbass regions, which continues at the time of writing this chapter.

Over the years, Oksana and I have continued our friendship against the backdrop of the situation in her region. Oksana told me about the day-to-day life in Alchevsk and how people pulled together not only to boost morale, and to give some sense of community to those living in the area, but also to help in the battle for survival in this war-torn region. In our conversations at that time, she recalled what a difficult time it was in 2014 – nobody had any money, and pensioners couldn't claim their pensions from Ukraine[31]. Banks closed and everyday necessities such as provisions and toiletries disappeared from the shop shelves[32]. The post offices in the region stopped functioning so there was nowhere for anybody to withdraw any money. To make matters worse, everyday products, which did appear sporadically in shops, were sold at highly inflated prices. People couldn't afford goods at such high prices.

I decided to interview Oksana about her voluntary work with *Food for Life* and what her motivations were for helping to set up the charity. What follows is the content of this interview from 2016. The original interview was in Russian, and I translated it into English[33].

**Oksana's story**

**TWB:** Why did you decide to become a *Food for Life* volunteer?

**Oksana:** *I started to volunteer for Food for Life back in 2014 when our region was occupied by the Russian forces. I was very depressed by the whole situation, lack of food in shops, running water only three times a week. You know that I was a teacher before the occupation and lost many students as a result of the aggression. Some of my friends died, my sister became internally displaced when she left the region with her family. I can't even see my mother because it is too dangerous for her to leave her home.*

*I saw there were many people with bigger problems than mine, people who had lost limbs due to mines, lonely, elderly people whose families had fled. I decided to sign up with Food for Life and never looked back. I enjoy delivering hot meals to the elderly and disabled. They are always so happy to see me and me too. My work is so important.*

*Since the escalation of the war this year, it was difficult and dangerous to get out and continue working, but I managed and now we are providing food for those displaced in our regions. It's really terrible, but by helping others, it keeps me going.*

**TWB:** When was *Food for Life* set up in Alchevsk?

**Oksana:** *Food for Life Alchevsk[34] was set up in October 2014 to provide help for people in need, such as pensioners, invalids, and families with many children. In the beginning, we were a really small-scale organisation, there were only five of us. We decided to set up the organisation in this region because people living here were not receiving any money from anywhere. Pensioners weren't receiving any pension money from Ukraine and at that time Russia wasn't providing any money to us. People couldn't buy food. It was a really difficult time. So, our small team of volunteers decided to help. Helping others in need gave us a sense of purpose.*

**TWB:** How does this organisation help these people?

**Oksana:** *We get help from Food for Life to provide meals for those in need. The food donations mainly* *come from Russia and Ukraine as well as from local businessmen. Those we help typically get two courses, which might include pea soup, maybe with macaroni or borscht. For the second course, there are usually different types of kasha [buckwheat] with carrots or other types of vegetables and bread rolls. Each day we make 150 litres of soup, kasha, and hand out 300 bread rolls. We feed the people and distribute food. People come to us at the canteen, which the state provides free of charge, and they receive food vouchers for three meals per week. On the other days they have to feed themselves and have to buy the food elsewhere and prepare it. We have the equipment at the canteen to prepare the food, which is also provided by Food for Life. So, we have volunteers who cook, give out the food and others who take it to those less able to get to the canteen, for example, invalids, the blind.*

*We work in the canteen for three days a week and on the other three days, some of our volunteers operate a mobile kitchen from a van we bought from funding that Food for Life provided.*

**TWB:** Does the organisation provide any other type of help in the region?

**Oksana:** *It provides different types of medicine, for example, for high blood pressure. Medicine is extremely expensive, and people have no money for medicine. Pensioners only receive about 3000 rubles per month, and they need to pay for their utility bills out of this. More than a third of this goes on bills, medicine is expensive, maybe they pay a minimum of 1000 (rubles) for medicines, maybe even 5000 a month. After they have paid for all of this, they do not have enough left for food. If a person lives in their own home, then it is even more expensive because of gas and electricity. The organisation has also provided prams for women with children.*

*We also put on charitable events for children, for example, we prepare New Year's fairy tales, put on plays. The volunteers put on events in the territorial centres for orphans, families with many children, sometimes in schools. We even go to Luhansk to perform our stories in Sunday schools. The stories are about magic (typical stories for kids). We write our own plays and stories. We play games with the children, put on competitions for them as well as sporting competitions in the towns. The families and children we visit are always really grateful and once they made us an enormous cake! It was 1.5 metres wide!*

**TWB:** What is your role within this organisation?

**Oksana:** *I help preparing food and taking food to those who cannot make it to the canteen. I used to volunteer four to five hours three days per week, but I do it less often now. I spend some of my time with those who I take food to. One of the people I visit is an 87-year-old woman who lives alone. She has no family, nobody at all and eighteen years ago she moved into this flat. She has been on crutches for eighteen years. She fell over, hurt her hip, and was bedridden, she couldn't do anything or go anywhere. So, I go to her flat, take her a meal, and help her to write letters. We have definitely helped to improve peoples' lives, especially children.*

**TWB:** What does the regional government do for these people?

**Oksana:** *It has provided us with the stolovaia [canteen] and some food, but not much. Sometimes it provides gifts for the children. Hospitals provide free medicine for those in hospital and the patients are fed.*

*Children in schools in first grade get a free meal. Children in other grades have to pay.*

**TWB:** Do you only help people in your town, or do you go to other towns or villages?

**Oksana:** *In August 2014, when the trubles began, we concentrated on helping people only in our town. Then in 2015, when we bought the van, we were able to go further afield into the countryside and other regions to help others suffering from the war. We prepared the food at home and took it to these people in big vats using the van. We did this for a year during the worst of the trubles.*

**TWB:** Have you ever come up against any dangerous situations while providing help?

**Oksana:** *In our town there hasn't been too much suffering because there is an enormous metallurgy plant here, which is very important to the region. There was shooting here only once. However, we go to places where there has been much suffering and where people have died, in the countryside, for example, where peace-abiding citizens were killed. We saw all the houses, which were destroyed by bombs and shooting,* and the destruction.... *We saw memorials to people who had perished, including children, with our own eyes. We saw the consequences of the war not far from our own area.*

**TWB:** Were you afraid when visiting these areas?

**Oksana:** *Of course, but we went there after all of this had happened. We saw tanks and houses that had been completely destroyed and met people who were the relatives of those who had died. We really wanted to help them in some way or another. They were so grateful for the help we provided with the food.*

**TWB:** How do you find out about these people who need help?

**Oksana:** *City organisations in the territorial centres provide lists of those needing help, including those who don't have any family or relatives, invalids, and families with many children. Our organisation got hold of the list and we started to help. Nowadays, we have an online presence where people can find us (VKontakte). We also need to show our sponsors what we are doing with the donated money, so we put what we were doing online. Also, it is an advert for those* who would like to help. *Unfortunately, many people in the photos on the website have died.*

**TWB:** Which other organisations help in this region?

**Oksana:** *Dobrye Ruki donate clothes, the Red Cross are also here and distribute food. Humanitarian aid organisations also appeared in the area and give help to single mothers, older people on their own, for example.*

*Other people who are not volunteers with a specific organisation help in their own way. My husband has his own business, like many others in Alchevsk. They help in other ways in the city, such as helping to rebuild houses and painting them.*

**TWB:** What does the future hold?

**Oksana:** *The organisation here has developed and will get bigger. The organisation has increased from five to forty members. Now, our organisation needs more donations. The situation with the organisation has changed right now and we are not getting as many donations as we used to. We are economising but need more money. We have an account where people can donate. 3000 rubles can feed ten people.*

*I feel that we have been forgotten though. We are not mentioned anywhere on the TV, in the media.*
*In the immediate future we still need help because the conflict is continuing. We need so much still.*

\*

In the summer of 2022, Oksana informed me that two of her *Food for Life* group members had lost their lives. They were in the *Food for Life* canteen in Alchevsk preparing food when a rocket hit the building. The two men died under the rubble.

\*

Since the escalation of the war in Ukraine on 24th February 2022, the United Nations estimates that 3.6 million people have been displaced within the country or have fled abroad. Millions of families have been left without a home, food, essentials such as water and electricity, safety, and security. Many have found it difficult to feed themselves and their families, putting themselves at risk of starvation and disease.

You may have seen the destruction caused to infrastructure by the constant missile bombings in the Luhansk and Donbass regions in eastern Ukraine.

People are risking their lives stepping outside of basements where they are sheltering to find food and water.

**Please help today by donating whatever you can: Go online using this address and donate today https://ffl.org/projects/response-to-crisis-in-ukraine**

# Endnotes

[1] Forsdick, Charles. "Vertical Travel" in Alasdair Pettinger and Tim Youngs (Eds.) *The Routledge Research Companion to Travel Writing*. Routledge, 2021.
[2] Urbain, Jean-Didier. *Ethnologue, mais pas trop* [Ethnography, but not excessively]. Éditions Payot & Rivages, 2003.
[3] Alpatov, V. M. *150 Iazykov i Politika 1917-1999: Sotsiolingvisticheskie Problemy SSSR i Postsovetskogo Prostranstva*. RAN, 1997; Laitin, David. *Identity in Formation: The Russian-Speaking Populations in the Near Abroad*. Cornell, 1998; Smith, Michael, G. *Language and Power in the Creation of the USSR: 1917-1953*. Mouton de Gruyter, 1998.
[4] Connor, Walker. *The National Question in Marxist-Leninist Theory and Strategy*. Princeton University Press. 1984, p.201.
[5] *Ibid.*, p.256.
[6] Grenoble, Lenore. *Language Policy in the Soviet Union*. Kluwer, 2003, p.43.
[7] Connor, Walker. *The National Question in Marxist-Leninist Theory and Strategy*. Princeton University Press, 1984, p.300-2.
[8] Smith, Michael, G. *Language and Power in the Creation of the USSR: 1917-1953*. Mouton de Gruyter, 1998, p.57.
[9] See Mikhailovskaia, quoted in Kirkwood, Michael. *Language Planning in the Soviet Union*. Macmillan, 1989.
[10] Kreindler, Isabelle. T. *Sociolinguistic Perspectives on Soviet National Languages: Their Past, Present and Future*. Mouton de Gruyter, 1989. p.58.
[11] See Anderson and Silver, quoted in Marshall, David F. 'A Politics of Language: Language as a Symbol in the Dissolution of the Soviet Union and Its Aftermath'. *International Journal of the Sociology of Language*, vol. 118, no. 1, 1996, Walter de Gruyter GmbH, https://doi.org10.1515/ijsl.1996.118.7, p.9.
[12] Grenoble, Lenore. *Language Policy in the Soviet Union*. Kluwer, 2003, p.206.
[13] Landau, Jacob. and Kellner-Heinkele, Barbara. *Politics of Language in the Ex-Soviet Muslim States*. Hurst and Company, 2001, p.58.
[14] Marshall, David F. 'A Politics of Language: Language as a Symbol in the Dissolution of the Soviet Union and Its Aftermath'. *International Journal of the Sociology of Language*, vol. 118, no. 1, 1996, Walter de Gruyter GmbH, https://doi.org10.1515/ijsl.1996.118.7, p.34.

[15] Norr, 1985, quoted in Landau, Jacob. and Kellner-Heinkele, Barbara. *Politics of Language in the Ex-Soviet Muslim States*. Hurst and Company, 2001, p.58.
[16] Khazanov, 1991 quoted in Landau, Jacob. and Kellner-Heinkele, Barbara. *Politics of Language in the Ex-Soviet Muslim States*. Hurst and Company, 2001, p.58.
[17] Marshall, David F. 'A Politics of Language: Language as a Symbol in the Dissolution of the Soviet Union and Its Aftermath'. *International Journal of the Sociology of Language*, vol. 118, no. 1, 1996, Walter de Gruyter GmbH, https://doi.org10.1515/ijsl.1996.118.7, p.33.
[18] See Anderson and Silver, quoted in Marshall, David F. 'A Politics of Language: Language as a Symbol in the Dissolution of the Soviet Union and Its Aftermath'. *International Journal of the Sociology of Language*, vol. 118, no. 1, 1996, Walter de Gruyter GmbH, https://doi.org10.1515/ijsl.1996.118.7, p.31.
[19] Marshall, David F. 'A Politics of Language: Language as a Symbol in the Dissolution of the Soviet Union and Its Aftermath'. *International Journal of the Sociology of Language*, vol. 118, no. 1, 1996, Walter de Gruyter GmbH, https://doi.org10.1515/ijsl.1996.118.7, p.33.
[20] See Horowitz quoted in Marshall, David F. 'A Politics of Language: Language as a Symbol in the Dissolution of the Soviet Union and Its Aftermath'. *International Journal of the Sociology of Language*, vol. 118, no. 1, 1996, Walter de Gruyter GmbH, https://doi.org10.1515/ijsl.1996.118.7, p.35.
[21] Государственная Третьяковская Галерея. *Оттепель*. 2017. [State Tret'iakov Gallery. Otepel'].
[22] Garipov, Y. and Faller, Helen. "The Politics of Language Reform and Bilingualism in Tatarstan". In Farimah Daftary and François Grin, (eds.) *Nation Building, Ethnicity and Language Politics on Transition Countries*. LGI/ECMI, 2003, pp.163-184; Graney, Katherine E. 'Education Reform in Tatarstan and Bashkortostan: Sovereignty Projects in Post-Soviet Russia'. *Europe-Asia Studies*, vol. 51, no. 4, Informa UK Limited, June 1999, pp. 611–632, https://doi.org10.1080/09668139998813, p.612; Yemelianova, Galina M. 'Shaimiev's "Khanate" on the Volga and Its Russian Subjects'. *Asian Ethnicity*, 2000, p.37.
[23] Brown, Keith E. (ed.) *Encyclopedia of Language & Linguistics*. Elsevier, 2006. p.509.
[24] Grenoble, Lenore. *Language Policy in the Soviet Union*. Kluwer. 2003, p.69.

[25] See 2010 Census Information http://www.tatstat.ru/VPN2010/DocLib8/%D0%BD%D0%B0%D1%86%20%D1%81%D0%BE%D1%81%D1%82%D0%B0%D0%B2.pdf.

[26] Iskhakova, Zaintunia. A. *Dvuiazychie v Gorodakh Tatarstana (1980-90-e gody)*. Fiker, 2001.

[27] Coalson, Bob. 'The Trauma of War: Homecoming after Afghanistan'. *Journal Humanistic Psychology*, vol. 33, no. 4, 1993, pp. 48–62.

[28] Danilova, Natalia. "The Case of Russia". *Armed Forces and Society*, vol. 36, no. 5, [Sage Publications, Ltd., Sage Publications, Inc.], 2010, pp. 890–916, https://www.jstor.org/stable/48608964.

[29] *Ibid.*

[30] See Turner, Paul. "Over 500,000 Hot Meals Served to Conflict Victims in Ukraine". 17 December 2016. www.ffl.org/9998/over-500000-hot-meals-served-to-conflict-victims-in-ukraine/.

[31] See Bojcun, Marko. "Why is the War in Eastern Ukraine still going on? 15 June 2016. www.opendemocracy.net/en/odr/why-is-war-in-eastern-ukraine-still-going-on/

[32] RFE/RL. "Life on the Frontline of the Ukraine Conflict". 14 January 2015. www.theguardian.com/world/2015/jan/14/-sp-life-civilians-front-line-ukraine-conflict.

[33] See the *Food for Life VKontakte* page: www.m.vk.com/@ffl_donbass-nasha-komanda.

**Further Reading**

As well as sources referred to in the endnotes of this book, below are some suggestions for further reading, which I have found useful in my research.

Faller, Helen. *Nation, Language, Islam: Tatarstan's Sovereignty Movement.* Central European Press, 2011.

Fishman, Joshua. *The Rise and Fall of the Ethnic Revival: Perspectives on Language and Ethnicity.* Mouton de Gruyter, 1985.

Forsyth, James. *The Caucasus: A History.* Cambridge University Press, 2013.

Gorter, Durk. Marten, Heiko, F. and Van Mensel, Luk. (eds.) *Minority Languages in the Linguistic Landscape.* Palgrave Macmillan, 2012.

May, Stephen. *Language and Minority Rights: Ethnicity, Nationalism and the Politics of Language.* Pearson Education Limited, 2001.

Plokhy, Sergii. *The Russo-Ukraine War.* Allen Lane, 2023.

Syutkin, Olga and Pavel. *CCCP Cook Book: True Stories of Soviet Cuisine*. Fuel, 2015.

Wigglesworth-Baker, Teresa. Language Planning and Power Politics in Post-Soviet Tatarstan. In *Language Planning in the Post-Communist Era: The Struggles for Language Control in the New Order in Eastern Europe, Eurasia and China*; Andrews, E., Ed.; Palgrave Macmillan, 2015.

Wigglesworth-Baker, Teresa. (2016) Russian-Titular Language Use in Post-Soviet Society: Effects of Language Policy in the Republic of Tatarstan. In *Nation-building and Identity in the Post-Soviet Space: New Tools and Approaches*; Isaacs, I and Polese, A.; Routledge, 2016.

Wigglesworth-Baker, T. 'Multilingual Education in Post-Soviet Georgia: Discourses of Ethnic Minority Integration'. *The Journal of Language Policy*, vol. 17, no. 3, Aug. 2018, pp. 285–306, https://doi.org10.1007/s10993-016-9426-y.

Wigglesworth-Baker, Teresa. 'Language Policy and Post-Soviet Identities in Tatarstan'.

*Nationalities Papers*, vol. 44, no. 1, Jan. 2016, pp. 20–37, https://doi.org10.1080/00905992.2015.1046425.

Wilson, Andrew. *The Ukrainians: Unexpected Nation*. Yale University Press, 2009.

Wilson, Andrew. *Ukraine Crisis: What it means for the West*. Yale University Press, 2014.

Zygar, Mikhail. *All the Kremlin's Men: Inside the Court of Vladimir Putin*. Public Affairs, 2016.

**Author bio**

Dr Teresa Wigglesworth-Baker is an academic, writer, and translator. She has written numerous articles on language and education policy in the post-Soviet space that have been published in international peer-reviewed journals and as chapters in edited volumes.

Teresa has travelled, worked, and researched extensively within the post-Soviet space. She had her first encounter with the Russian language at school and has never looked back since. Her first trip was to the Soviet Union in 1984 when her school held an exchange trip to Leningrad, Donetsk and Moscow. Following on from this, she continued studying Russian at university and holds a PhD in Russian and Slavonic Studies. Teresa has worked in Russia, Poland and the Czech Republic and has carried out research in the Republic of Tatarstan, an autonomous republic situated within the geopolitical territory of the Russian Federation and Georgia, a former Soviet state.

Teresa has taught for many years in higher education. She has taught many subjects including Russian, French, and English languages, social science, the arts and humanities. She is an accomplished musician and plays the recorder and saxophone. She is currently learning the accordion.

Teresa also began painting during the lockdown of 2020. Many of her paintings have been inspired by her travels to the post-Soviet space.

The cover artwork is by Teresa.

Printed in Great Britain
by Amazon